3.11 67 7/07

5/2/90

Palo Alto City Library

THE COMPLETE BOOK OF BUDGERIGARS

THE COMPLETE BOOK OF BUDGERIGARS

STAN and BARBARA MOIZER

Foreword by Alf Ormerod

American Consulting Editor
Matthew M. Vriends, PhD

BARRON'S
New York

All inquiries should be addressed to:
Barron's Educational Series, Inc.
250 Wireless Boulevard
Hauppauge, New York 11788

International Standard Book No. 0–8120–6059–8
Library of Congress No.88–3459

Library of Congress Cataloging in Publication Data
Moizer, Stan.
     Budgerigars: a complete guide.
     1. Budgerigars. I. Moizer, Barbara. II. Vriends, Matthew. III. Title.
SF473.B8M65 1988   636.6′864   88–3459
ISBN 0–8120–6059–8

Front cover: Normal grey cock, by Dennis Avon (Ardea London)
Inside photo credits: Color photographs are by Angela Moss.
Black and white photographs are by the authors, with
additional pictures from the following (on pages indicated):
Ardea UK Ltd 142, J. Benson 134, Camera Press 102, 136,
G. Clarke 72, J. Densley 130, Fox Photos 103, A. Francis
56, A. A. Kent 21 bottom, Harry Lacey 67, 88 bottom, 109, 111,
D. B. Nicholls 41, Portsmouth and Sunderland Newspapers Ltd 48,
Southern Aviaries 135, Tony Tilford 20, 35, 37,
43, 69 (both), 79 bottom, 120, 138.

Acknowledgments: The authors would like to thank the following for
giving permission for their birds to be photographed: Steve Amos and
Ron Thumwood, Don Ashby, Jeff Attwood, Harry Bryan, Eric and Mike
Lane, Aubrey Punter and Bill Saundry. Gratitude is also expressed to all
who helped in the preparation of this book, including the American
Budgerigar Society, Dr John Baker, A. R. Bayliss, Arthur Bracey, Ray
Brown, the UK Budgerigar Society, Sherrill Capi, Graham Clarke, B. H.
Coles BV Sc. MRVS, Stephen Dew, Framed Philatelics, Rodney Harris,
Bernard Kellett, Linden Artists (Steve Lings and Brian Watson), Les
Lockey, Angela Moss, Alf Ormerod, Cyril Rogers and Graham Tann.

Editor: Lesley Young
Designer: Carole Perks
Typeset by Deltatype Ltd, Ellesmere Port
Reprographics by Fotographics Ltd, London–Hong Kong
Printed in Portugal by Printer Portuguesa Industria Grafica Lda

CONTENTS

Foreword

I have known Stan and Barbara Moizer for a number of years and feel sure it would be difficult to find a couple more dedicated to the hobby of breeding and exhibiting budgerigars. Between them they have had many years of practical experience and they are both very actively engaged in helping in the administration of the Budgerigar Society. Their intimate knowledge of the budgerigar fancy is aptly demonstrated in this book, which is laid out in an easy to follow alphabetical style.

Newcomers will find a fund of information on all aspects of the hobby in this book, written in simple language and carefully cross-referenced. Beginners who follow the advice on birdrooms, husbandry and breeding will have a sound basis from which to start. All aspects of exhibiting, the status rules, and show procedure have been meticulously covered to ensure that the relative newcomer can understand the path he or she should follow on the road to success in the show scene. With this book as a guide and with the patience and dedication that is so necessary in this hobby, there is no reason why the beginner should not eventually breed the outstanding specimens which are the aim of every serious breeder.

The budgerigar has changed a great deal over the years from the wild birds first brought over from Australia – and they are still changing. A book which brings the knowledge of all these changes up to date is a necessity and this book succeeds in that object.

For the experienced fancier, the book gives an opportunity to compare the various recommendations of the authors with his or her own routine and perhaps he or she will find that some of the ideas can be blended in to advantage with his or her own methods.

Whether the reader is simply a bird lover or a dedicated breeder and exhibitor, he or she will be delighted with the superb color photographs of some of today's leading exhibition budgerigars; pictures which demonstrate the features so desirable in top show birds throughout the world.

I have read through this book several times and have no hesitation in recommending it to anyone who is interested in these little birds which have given me so much pleasure over so many years and have been the means of making friends in every corner of the globe. I hope it will serve to introduce many newcomers to our great hobby as well as supply new information to all experienced fanciers for whom a new book on budgerigars is a welcome occasion.

ALF ORMEROD

Introduction

Budgerigars are beautiful birds. They are available in myriad colors and pattern combinations; they are comparatively easy to manage and to breed; they adapt to almost any climatic conditions; they make affectionate and absorbing pets. Small wonder that these colorful parakeets have become so universally popular.

It was not always so. Until this century, they were virtually unknown outside their native Australia. When that country was discovered by Captain James Cook in 1770, one of the wonders reported was flocks of tiny parrots, so great in numbers that when they flew overhead they blotted out the sun for miles, and when they alighted on the branches of dead trees their brilliant green plumage gave the impression that the tree had been instantly resurrected and had broken into leaf.

Budgerigars were introduced to England by John Gould in 1840 and soon afterwards a few arrived in America. By the late 1880s, dealers were importing hundreds of thousands of pairs into Europe until, in 1894, the Australian government put a ban on the export of parakeets.

By this time, enthusiasts all over Europe were beginning to breed budgerigars and were so successful that the Australian ban had very little effect on the budgerigar population.

At first, all the birds were of the basic light green variety, but in 1870 the first color mutation appeared in Belgium, causing quite a sensation. It was described as a pure yellow bird with red eyes, and is presumed to have been a lutino. At the same time, yellow birds with black eyes and pale wing markings appeared. The breeders knew nothing of sex-linkage at that time and the lutino was "lost," but the black-eyed yellow variety was established.

Stories began to circulate of a budgerigar of incredible beauty. It was described as having a pure white face with a smooth, sky-blue body. It remained but a legend until, in 1910, two skyblues were shown at a bird show at the Horticultural Hall, London.

With the advent of the blue series birds, the Royal House of Japan became interested in budgerigars and were reputed to have paid astronomical sums for pairs of blue birds. Japanese nobility started the fashion of giving these lovely blue and white birds as "love tokens" and soon the fashion had spread to anyone who could afford the high prices being charged.

In 1927 the Japanese government banned the importation of budgerigars, but by this time the Japanese were breeding the birds themselves, and to this day, Japan has a strong following of budgerigar fanciers, and two national budgerigar associations.

After the skyblues came the dark greens which, when mated with the skyblues, produced cobalts, and then, as the hobby passed out of the hands of the few into the realms of the ordinary fanciers, the mutations multiplied until today's enormous variety was achieved.

This book has been produced to cover all aspects of interest in the budgerigar. Its alphabetical arrangements of subject should allow anyone to find an item of interest very speedily. Thus, the owner of a new pet who wishes to teach it to talk can turn immediately to *TALKING* and will find comprehensive instructions. The newcomer to showing budgerigars will find all of the essential information under such entries as *SHOW PROCEDURE*, *BABY SHOWS* and *OPEN SHOWS*. Because of widespread interest in British standards and practices, certain details that do not pertain in the US – e.g., *BEGINNER* – are also fully explained. For the experienced breeder wishing to renew or equip his birdroom, there are entries on *EQUIPMENT*, *BIRDROOMS*, *FLIGHTS* and many other subjects of interest. Anyone who has fallen under the spell of this most enchanting of birds will find this to be a book of absorbing interest.

A

ACCESSORIES
In addition to the birdroom or aviary, a number of items are required for breeding budgerigars. Some, such as seed hoppers and water fountains, will be in use throughout the year. Others, such as nest boxes, blocks and finger drawers for feeding soft food mixtures, are used only during the breeding season. Collectively these are known as accessories, but the most important items will be dealt with individually under the appropriate headings throughout the book.

ADDITIVES
This term is generally used to describe anything which is provided for the birds in addition to their normal food requirements (see *FEEDING*). It covers a huge range of products available from most good pet stores. A large number of these are added to the drinking water, but it cannot be stressed too strongly that when anything is added to the birds' drinking water, they have no choice but to take it, whereas if it is offered in a dry state they can ignore it if it is not wanted. Nature is often wiser than the breeder and the birds usually seem to know what is good for them and what is unnecessary.

One essential additive is iodine. This can be given in the form of iodine blocks which have the additional benefit of providing the birds with something to tear to pieces — which they undoubtedly enjoy. Iodine blocks can be obtained in small sizes intended for pet cages or in sizes for the pigeon trade, which are ideal for use in budgerigar flights or breeding cages.

Various *vitamin supplements* are available, but care must be taken not to overdose with any particular vitamin. Carefully check the ingredients of any of the multi-vitamin products and do not give any other product containing a similar ingredient. Most products sold for babies and young children are harmless to budgerigars. A good rule-of-thumb amount is that suggested for the smallest babies. If this is then added to the drinking fountain, the dilution results in a suitable dosage. Baby tonics can also be given in the same manner, but these should not be necessary if a good basic diet is provided. (See *MINERALS* and *VITAMINS*.)

ADDLED EGGS
Originally fertile, the embryos in these eggs die in the very early stage — before the seventh or eighth day. Research has shown that the reason for this is frequently the presence of bacteria which have been absorbed through the shell. The egg takes on a dark tinge and when opened has quite a foul smell. The bacteria can be transferred to the eggs from the hands of the breeder, and for this reason the less the eggs are handled, the better. (See also *INCUBATION*.)

AGE
When buying a budgerigar as a pet, it is most important to check that it is a young bird because it is very difficult to tame or teach an adult bird to talk. In the normal varieties, the greens, blues, greys, etc., it is simple to tell if a budgerigar is under three months old, by observing the front of the head. Until the baby budgerigar has been through its first molt (usually between three and four months old), it has a series of *striations* across the top of the head from above the eyes. These birds are known as *barheads*. This method of deciding age cannot be used with varieties which have no markings, such as albinos and lutinos.

Another method of checking is to look at the eyes. For at least the first three months of their lives, the baby budgerigars have no whites around the pupils of their eyes. The pupil, black in the case of normals and deep red or plum

A barhead budgerigar at 14 weeks of age. The bars, or striations, on the front of the head are just beginning to disappear.

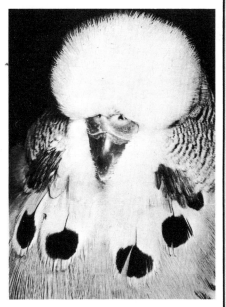

The head of an adult budgerigar has no bars.

colored in albinos, lutinos, fallows and lacewings, is all solid color with no white around the outside. There are exceptions to this rule, unfortunately. The recessive pied and dark-eyed clear varieties never develop the white iris rings around the pupils even in adulthood.

For breeding purposes it is always wise to buy *close-banded* birds. The band will give the code number of the breeder and the year in which the bird was banded. If a bird is over three years old, while it might breed, there is always a doubt, and in any case it will not continue to breed in later years.

The average age of a budgerigar in the wild is probably about two or three years. A pet bird, however, can live well into its teens if well looked after.

AILMENTS AND DISEASES

In general, budgerigars are healthy little creatures and most live their whole lives without suffering from any disease, but, as with all livestock, they are subject to a number of ailments and, being such small creatures, have not a great deal of resistance to illnesses. Prompt attention is very important. The first sign of trouble is usually finding a bird roosting on both feet with its head tucked under its wing. Pet owners should be aware that it is *normal* for a bird to perch on *one* foot with its head tucked under its

wing. If the plumage is fluffed out and the droppings are loose and watery, or green and slimy, it is a sure sign that all is not well. The bird should be removed at once and examined for injury. If none is obvious, then it should be put into either a hospital cage, or a show cage which can be placed near heat. If a hospital cage is used, the thermostat should be set at 27–30°C (80°–85°F). If a hospital cage is not available, then the show cage or a similar cage should be placed in front of a fire, fairly close to a radiator, or in any place which is both draft- and fume-free. Gas appliances are not advised. Do not put the cage where the bird will be too hot (see *HOSPITAL CAGE*). In addition to drinking water, a shallow bowl of water should be placed near the cage to provide humidity.

If the illness is minor, the most effective treatment is heat alone.

If the droppings are loose or green, very often the condition can be cured simply by substituting strong cold tea (without milk or sugar) for drinking water. This has an astringent effect and is soothing when the alimentary system has been inflamed for any reason. There are several proprietary brands of medicines available for the treatment of *diarrhea* and *enteritis* and these should be used as directed on the bottle or packet. It is wise to check that these medicines have a fresh smell and have not been in stock for a long time in the pet store.

Anal prolapse or prolapse of the oviduct is another condition from which breeding hens can suffer. This seldom occurs if the seed provided during the breeding season is mixed with a very small amount of cod liver oil emulsion (see *FEEDING*). This condition is usually caused by the bird's attempting to expel either a soft-shelled egg or a particularly large egg. Very rarely it can be the result of *constipation*.

The symptoms are fluffed feathers, tail held high, swelling around the vent, giving the appearance of the bird being "blown up," while in severe cases part of the intestine may protrude from the vent.

The bird should be removed from the breeding cage and caged alone. Veterinary attention should be obtained immediately, as the treatment is usually surgical in nature (to hold the oviduct in, stitches are placed in the cloaca, or if the oviduct is severely damaged, it must be surgically removed). If professional help is unavailable, gently soak and bathe the prolapse in cold 1 percent saline solution and cotton wool, and push it back into the abdomen very gently. First wash the hands really thoroughly, then smear the finger liberally with a lubricating jelly or cream, then gently try to maneuver the protruding part back into place. If an egg can be felt, the bird should be placed back in the breeding cage and kept warm until the egg is passed.

The bird should be given a few days' rest alone and its seed mixed with a minute quantity of cod liver oil, or liquid paraffin. It is advisable that this bird should not be used for breeding purposes until the following breeding season and then that a careful watch should be kept.

Coccidiosis is said to be a rare disease in budgerigars, but it occurred at one time in one of the authors' aviaries. The first sign was pink drops of liquid, about the size of a thumbnail, on the floor of the flight. A bird looked sick and was placed in a warm spot. The droppings were pink, as though a small amount of blood was present. They were pure liquid with no solid at all. The bird did not seem fluffed up as is normal with sick birds, but it was not eating and seemed lethargic. Within hours another had evinced the same symptoms. By the following morning, four more were in the same condition. A vet, called in, could not give an explanation, but took some of the liquid droppings for examination. Then the first bird to show the signs died. The body was taken to the vet without delay and the following day coccidiosis was diagnosed. The whole flock was treated with sulphadimidine and although about twenty began to show blood in their droppings, there were no more deaths. The sick birds recovered and there seemed to be no loss of fertility in the stock at the next breeding season. The birds were moved temporarily and the whole aviary was stringently cleaned and disinfected before they were allowed back in.

Coccidia is a parasite which lays eggs in the intestines and penetrates the mucous lining. The eggs, called *oocysts*, are passed in the droppings and can be picked up and swallowed by another bird. They multiply in the gut and eventually produce more oocysts. Because of the budgerigar's habit of eating old droppings, this cycle makes the disease very infectious within the stud.

FRENCH MOLT is the most perplexing and exasperating disease which affects budgerigars. This condition is dealt with under its own heading.

"*Going light*" is another perplexing condition which causes a great deal of concern among breeders. It is used to describe a budgerigar which, although apparently fit and eating well, continues to lose weight until the breastbone can be felt, sharp and without its normal covering of muscle and fat. Without treatment, the bird eventually dies.

Research into this condition has

revealed that in the majority of cases, the villi, which are fine projections in the intestine, have become shorter, or have fused together, and this prevents the bird from absorbing the nutrients from the seed it eats. Tests have indicated that this condition can often be caused by allergies to certain foods, some possible sources being soaked oats, hard-boiled eggs, or some of the more exotic seeds. It is recommended that birds going light should be given a very simple diet of plain canary seed, greens and pure water. An antibiotic is available to treat this condition, but it would be necessary to continue the treatment for the rest of the bird's life. Since it is not recommended that these birds should be used for breeding, and they would need to be caged separately, this seems impractical. However, pet owners could try to keep their birds healthy by offering a plain diet and by dosing with the antibiotic, sodium cromoglycate. As with any antibiotic, it is wise to seek advice from an experienced veterinarian on dosage. There are many excellent avian veterinarians in this country. For one in your area, contact the Association of Avian Veterinarians, P.O. Box 299, East Northport, New York 11731 (5,16/757–6320).

Vomiting in budgerigars is usually caused by a disease known as *trichomoniasis*. Owners of pets should not confuse this with the very normal behavior of *regurgitating seed*. Vomiting is far more violent and usually results in the feathers above and below the beak becoming matted. This disease can be transmitted to other birds by beak to beak contact, which includes feeding chicks. Effective treatments are dimetriolazole (Emtryl) or metronidazole (Flagyl) as prescribed by your veterinarian. Excess dosage can be dangerous, therefore the amount should not be exceeded and the treatment given for seven days. Even though the vomiting has ceased, the treatment should be continued for the full seven days to prevent a resistance being built up to the antibiotic.

Fungi are the cause of *aspergillosis* and *candidiasis*. Fungi are airborne spores which land mainly on vegetable matter and cause mold to form. If you leave a moist loaf of bread around for a day or so, you can watch the molds forming. The best prevention of fungal disease in your budgerigars is to keep their surroundings clean and dry and to remove all moist food or greens which have not been eaten the same day. Candidiasis usually occurs in the mouth or crop. The mold, mixed with dead tissue, builds into a cheese-like mass which partially blocks the organ. Birds are usually treated with fungicidal antibiotics and injections of vitamin A, but very often the diagnosis is not made until the condition has progressed too far for a cure to be effected.

The *aspergillus* fungus affects the air sacs and lungs of the bird, but provided that the bird is fit and vigorous, it should be able to overcome the disease before it reaches dangerous proportions. A vet may well advise treatment with an antibiotic, but this should not be given without expert advice.

Other diseases caused by fungus spores are *skin lesions*, such as *ringworm*. The signs to look for are loss of feather, exposing the skin which looks grey and scaly, or moist and yellow, and covered with a film which can be removed to show the skin slightly spotted with blood. The budgie is likely to scratch or rub the spot until it is raw and bleeding if it is not treated. Treatment with an anti-fungal cream is essential and must be continued until every trace of the lesion has disappeared. (See also *CHLAMYDIA* .)

ALBINOS
The albino is a variety of budgerigar which appears to be pure white. It is, in fact, a blue series bird which is carrying the *albino factor*. This factor has the effect of removing all color from the bird. The eyes are deep red with a white iris ring, and the feet and legs are fleshy pink.

AUTOMATIC WATERING SYSTEM

Probably the most time-saving equipment which can be installed in a birdroom is an automatic watering system. It cuts out the necessity for drinking fountains and the daily chore of filling them, and ensures that the drinking water is always fresh. This system, which is widely used in the USA, consists of a pressure-reducing valve. This is a unit which is connected to the domestic water supply and reduces the water pressure. The water is routed to the cages and flights via a black PVC tube. (Black tubing is used to prevent any growth of algae which would occur in a transparent tube.) Tee pieces are used to supply the individual cages and flights. At the end of each tube there is a drinking outlet for the birds. This consists of a non-returnable valve with a stem which is moved by the birds. When the stem moves from the central position, pure, fresh tap water is released. Budgerigars are very inquisitive and learn how to operate this system of water supply very quickly. When it is newly installed, it usually takes less than an hour for them to discover that pressing the valve delivers their water supply.

Two possible sources of danger, which should be watched for, are that the room should always be above freezing point, otherwise, just as in any water supply, the tiny pipes could freeze; and if for any reason, such as rebuilding, you need to break down the system, care must be taken to check, once it has been reassembled, that it is fully operative again. To do this, press down the center stem at each outlet to make certain that the water is running freely. It takes so little time to do this that it is a good idea to make it part of your daily routine. It is not necessary to check each individual outlet every day — just one from each run of piping would be quite sufficient. (See also *WATER*.)

AUTOPSY

When an unknown disease affects a number of budgerigars in a flock, pointing to the likelihood of its being an infectious disease, unfortunately the most accurate diagnosis usually depends upon a detailed autopsy. Birds which have been dead for six hours or more are seldom of use for diagnosing bacterial disease. The fancier should therefore try to provide the veterinary surgeon with birds which appear to be in the terminal stages of the illness. Although this may seem harsh, and a breeder is always loath to lose birds which may well be those he most prizes,

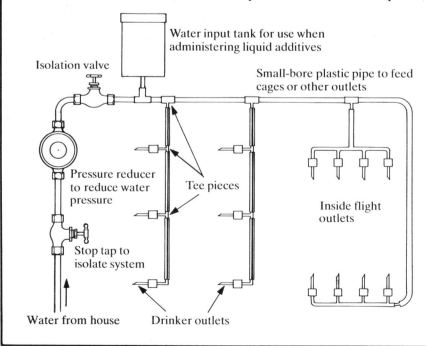

Water input tank for use when administering liquid additives

Isolation valve

Small-bore plastic pipe to feed cages or other outlets

Pressure reducer to reduce water pressure

Tee pieces

Inside flight outlets

Stop tap to isolate system

Water from house   Drinker outlets

An automatic watering system.

it is better to sacrifice one or two birds, which in any case seem unlikely to recover, than to lose a large part of the stud through an undiagnosed disease.

The more autopsies that are carried out, the more is learned about the causes of death and disease in our birds. Anyone who experiences a number of unexplained deaths is advised to take some of the dead birds to the local vet for a post mortem, and the sooner after death these can be taken, the more likely is the vet to be able to pinpoint the cause.

One of the authors had an experience at one time which impressed upon him the importance of autopsies. One bird died, then another. He was unhappy about losing birds, but since they do suffer from heart attacks, strokes and most of such similar diseases in humans, he accepted the losses. When more died he suspected some form of poisoning. All the seed in stock was discarded and new supplies brought in. Every inch of the birdroom was checked for possible mice infestation and the birds were observed diligently. Still no clue was found: the birds appeared healthy and active and then they died. He took a couple along to the vet for an autopsy and what was found were specks of galvanizing from the wire netting. Rust had penetrated underneath the galvanizing of the wire mesh and the birds had picked if off. As soon as the wire netting had been changed, there was no further trouble.

AVIARIES

For bird lovers, a garden aviary can supply unending pleasure as they sit and watch the antics of budgerigars at play, marvelling at the variety of their colors. A very small outlay is needed to provide a garden with this focal point which will prove popular with family, friends and visitors alike.

Although planning permission may not always be required for building a garden aviary, it is both a wise and friendly gesture to check first with neighbors to be certain that there will be no objection to the noise of the birds.

The simplest and most basic type of garden aviary consists of an open flight fitted with sleeping quarters. A rigid framework is covered with wire netting or weldmesh.

Ideally, the aviary should have a sound concrete base with a slight slope to allow rain to run off, but if no base is to be provided, then the aviary needs to be pegged very firmly into the ground.

Once the flight is completed, secure sleeping quarters are necessary. They can be very primitive as long as they are secure, and could consist, virtually, of a four-sided wooden box, with the top covered, leaving the bottom open.

A window is needed at the back to allow light into the quarters and to allow you to see the birds. Two or three perches should be firmly fixed, lengthways, inside the box.

Another simple method of constructing sleeping quarters is to have a complete box with a window in the rear wall. The front, which faces into the flight, is made into an opening door to facilitate cleaning. Two entrance holes, about 5 cm (2 in) in diameter, need to be cut in the door to allow the birds to enter and leave the sleeping quarters. As with the four-sided box, perches need to be fitted firmly.

It is wise to clean, scrape and wash all floors weekly to avoid any build-up of droppings. Cleaning is made easier if sawdust or shavings are sprinkled on the floor of the sleeping quarters, and if there is a concrete base to the aviary, a liberal spreading of coarse sand (washed clean of salt) both simplifies cleaning and enhances its appearance.

A flight 2-2.5 m (6-8 ft) long, a minimum of 0.9 m (3 ft) wide and 2 m (6 ft) high would be suitable for about 20 to 25 birds.

The framework can be made from 4 × 4 cm (1½ × 1½ in) lumber or from hard plastic tubing. If lumber is used it will be necessary to treat it with a *nontoxic* wood preservative prior to fitting

Diagram of a garden aviary with two flights.
1 Covered-in sleeping quarters (must be rain-proof) 2 Glass window 3 Feed board 4 Doors 5 Aperture for birds to enter and leave 6 Perches 7 Food tray 8 Covered roof 9 Door to other flight 10 Safety porch 11 Outer door.

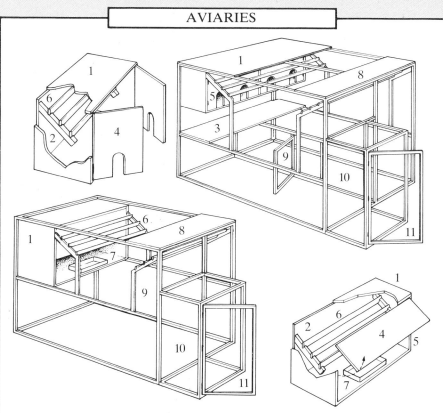

the wire netting. The framework, both top and sides, should be totally covered with heavy-gauge wire netting or weldmesh to prevent the birds escaping and to protect them against cats, children and vermin. All the wire netting should be painted with black *asphalt* paint, inside and out, as protection. The roof should be partially covered with a solid material to give the birds somewhere to shelter from the sun. It can be boarded and felted, or covered with an asbestos sheet or anything similar. The remainder of the roof needs to be covered with lightweight plastic to protect the budgerigars from the droppings of wild birds, which could be a source of infection.

Grass is not a good floor for the flight. It is very quickly eaten away by the birds, and the ground, particularly under the perches, will become sour. If no floor has been built in, then it is a good idea to fork over the ground lightly, but regularly. The birds like to break up the newly forked ground, either for enjoyment or when seeking grubs, insects and natural minerals. It is unwise to plant any type of shrub or tree inside the flight because it would quickly be

stripped of bark and leaves. For safe access to the sleeping quarters or flight, a safety door will be necessary. A description of its construction will be found under *SAFETY DOOR*.

There are many forms of aviaries which can be bought ready made, ranging from very simple to elaborate and decorative structures, but however well these might complement the garden landscape, the welfare of the birds must be of primary importance. The rules given for a simple aviary must still be complied with.

It is very important that if you do not intend to breed birds you must never put anything resembling a nest box into the aviary as this would cause jealousy and fighting among the hens. Perhaps, in this case, it might be more sensible to keep only cocks, for there is seldom any squabbling among a flock of cocks. Once hens are introduced, however, especially when they are coming into breeding condition, then the hens are apt to fight for their partners and their territory.

B

BABY SHOWS

These shows are usually sponsored by local clubs to enable their members to discover whether they have bred any birds with particular show potential, and also whether their fellow members have had successful breeding seasons. The emphasis at these shows is on the youngsters which still have their first feathers, those with which they left the nest. In the case of the normal varieties they will still be showing their barred heads, and with others the eyes will not yet be showing the white iris rings. Sometimes, with smaller clubs, there will not be sufficient entries to warrant holding a show

exclusively for nest feather birds, and they will schedule classes for the older birds too. This happens particularly with cage bird societies which also cater to canaries and other varieties. Newcomers to the hobby, who might wish to exhibit their older birds, should check first with the club as to what classes are being scheduled.

BANDING A CHICK

The *closed coded band* should be placed on the bird's leg when it is between five and ten days old. It is better to put the band on early and risk having it come off and need to be put on again, than to leave it until the foot is too big for the band to slip over and thus to risk hurting the chick.

It is important that your hands are kept warm when banding chicks because they have been taken from beneath a warm hen in a warm nest box and the shock of being held in freezing cold hands

Two methods of banding a chick; with two toes facing forward and two facing back: or with three facing forward and one facing back.

1. The two forward, two back method.

a) Place band over two front toes.

b) Pull the long rear toe through with a toothpick or pointed matchstick.

c) Pull short rear toe through leaving band just above ankle joint.

d) Band in position.

2. The three forward method.

a) Gather the three long toes together.

b) Place band over three long toes and gently push band over ball of foot.

c) Carefully pull the short toe through to clear the band.

d) Band in position.

Stage 1

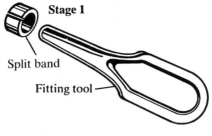

Split band

Fitting tool

Stage 2

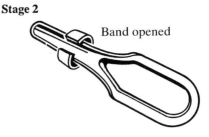

Band opened

Stage 3

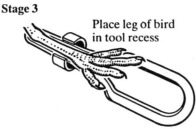

Place leg of bird
in tool recess

Stage 4

Withdraw the ringing tool.
Band now closes
around bird's leg.

Fitting a split band
on the leg of a
budgerigar.

could be fatal. Those who suffer from cold hands should have hot water, a hot radiator or even a hot water bottle available for warming their hands before beginning to carry out the task of banding chicks.

The operation of banding a chick can be quite frightening to a raw beginner. It is worth while practicing at first on a chick whose legs are too small to hold a band. The band will slide on easily and can be gently pulled off again without causing any damage or pain to the little baby bird.

There are two methods of banding a bird in current use. The first is to take the two toes which face forward, place the band over these and carry on until the band is over the first joint, then, with an instrument with a blunt point, such as the end part of a small plastic knitting needle, a blunted toothpick or a used match with the head removed and the end cut into a point, first pull the large back toe through the band, followed by the smaller back toe. The band will then be positioned on the leg above the first joint.

The second method is to hold the two forward-facing toe and the small backward-facing toe together, place the band over all three, and then over the first joint. As described above, the one large backward-facing toe is then pulled through the ring with the blunt-pointed instrument. At this age the

feet have not properly formed and holding a toe in the wrong direction is not painful or harmful, but remember that they are tender little things, the skin is soft, and gentleness is very important.

BANDS

Closed coded bands are a permanent means of identifying a bird. The band is made from dyed aluminum and the color changes each year. Therefore it is possible to look at birds flying around with, say, purple bands on their legs and immediately identify them as having been hatched in 1987. The bands are issued by the ruling body in most countries where budgerigars are bred and exhibited. In the US this is the American Budgerigar Society; in the UK, the Budgerigar Society. The year of issue, followed by the serial number of the bird and then the code number of the breeder is stamped on each one.

Split bands, as their name implies, can be opened and therefore can be placed on the bird's leg when it is an adult. They can be obtained in most colors, or in a combination of colors, and are used to identify families. When a breeder specializes in a certain color — say, blue — he or she might have a flight full of blue birds and have difficulty in identifying individual birds. By using a distinctive colored split band for each different family, he or she can immediately pick out related birds.

Although split bands can be put on the leg at any age of a bird's life, if they are being used for the purpose of identifying a family, they are best put on before the young are taken away from their parents. It is a simple task as, when the bands are bought, a banding tool is supplied. The band is slipped onto the tool with the split in line with the groove, the leg of the bird is laid in the tool and the tool is then withdrawn along the leg, leaving the band attached. If the band has not quite closed up tightly after being stretched, it can be closed quite easily with thumb and finger.

BARHEADS

This is a term used to describe young budgerigars before they have been through their first molt, which usually takes place at the age of three to four months. Until they have molted their nest feathers, budgerigar chicks of the normal varieties have *bars*, or *striations*, across the front of their heads. Once the nest feathers molt, the new feathers are of a clear color, either yellow or white, depending on whether the bird is of the green or blue series.

BATHS

Although it is not essential for budgerigars to bathe, most enjoy it and it is good for them. It encourages them to preen their feathers which helps to give them the bloom that is essential for show winners. Care should be taken never to provide too deep a bath because the birds can drown in water over about 4 cm (1½ in) deep. The bowls must be removed once the birds have used them, to prevent them being fouled by droppings and becoming a potential health hazard. For pet cages, plastic baths which fit on to the opening can be obtained and they will provide hours of entertainment for both pet and owner. If the pet bird is loath to enter a bath for the first time, it can be encouraged by putting at the far side any tidbit of which it is fond — a piece of millet spray, greens or sweet apple will usually entice it in. Many pet budgies delight in bathing under a cold tap which has been left dribbling — but the owner must make absolutely certain that all doors and windows are closed and no stove burners are turned on (or still hot) before releasing the pet in the kitchen.

BEAKS

The beak does not become really hard until the budgerigar is about three weeks old. During this time it is most important that it should not be distorted by the accumulation of caked food. The beak should be examined daily and any trapped food should be removed gently with a blunt matchstick or toothpick. (See *UNDERSHOT BEAK*.)

A plastic bath which fits over the opening to the budgerigar cage.

The normal varieties

Normal dark green cock.

Violet budgerigar on a Capern's card. (These cards were issued by the makers of Capern's birdseed.)

Normal violet hen.

Magnificent normal
grey cock with
outstanding head
qualities.

BEGINNER

In the United States and several other countries, no beginner classes are scheduled; exhibitors go directly into novice classes. In some smaller shows in the UK this is also true and in this case beginners may enter the novice classes and then revert to beginner classes when these are scheduled. Much confusion arises from the fact that exhibitors may remain beginners for the rest of their lives *if they never enter in open shows*.

The BS (UK) rule is that a beginner may show in this section these are awarded (in the UK) at shows at a lower patronage level. A very similar system exists in the US. For the purpose of obtaining a *champion bird certificate*, nine best of color certificates, at least three of which must be won in adult classes, would be needed (or two challenge certificates and three best of color certificates, or one challenge certificate and six best of color certificates). Three best of color certificates are equal to one challenge certificate. A best of color certificate can be won with an unbanded bird, but in this case the

The authors' birdroom with its attached flight.

either for three years *or* until he or she has won four first prizes in *full* classes *at open shows — whichever is the longer period*. Full classes consist of at least seven exhibits shown by three different exhibitors and can be any age or breeder classes. For the purpose of counting these wins, one prize is counted for a win of a prize of best in section, provided three exhibitors are competing and there are seven exhibits in the lineup being judged.

BEST OF COLOR CERTIFICATES

Similar to *challenge certificates*, certificate would be marked to this effect and would not count towards a champion bird certificate. As with challenge certificates, the exhibitor must be a Budgerigar Society member, and have nominated BS on his entry form, to be eligible to win a best of color certificate.

BIRDROOMS

Basically, a birdroom is an enclosed building plus flights. The building can be an existing shed, unused garage, or barn, or it can be something built purposely as a birdroom. Whatever is used, there are certain basic requirements.

First, the building must be weatherproof. Any leaking from the roof must be stopped before the building can be used. Other than the discomfort that this can cause the fancier, more important is the comfort, safety and hygiene of the birds. Water could seep into the nest boxes and literally drown the baby chicks, or it could soak the nesting material, causing discomfort and possibly serious illness in the hen. It might soak into materials which could cause molds to be released into the air and inhaled by the birds. Every leak and potential leak must be eliminated.

The next task is to draw up a plan giving the location of cages, flights, storage area, windows and the entrance door into the birdroom. The drawings on page 25 show a suggested plan which can be followed if the building is being newly built, or modified where necessary for an existing building.

In colder areas it is preferable that the birdroom and flights face south to catch all the warmth of any sun there is during the spring period when the youngsters are most likely to be using the flights. Flights facing north-east should be avoided if it is humanly possible, as these would catch the coldest and most biting of the winter winds. Although budgies are hardy little creatures, they seem to have no instinct which tells them to shelter from cold winds.

If the birdroom is built of lumber, always try to allow for later expansion, for most fanciers find that they wish to expand their first birdroom as their interest, and their stock, grows. Even if a building is being adapted, it is often possible to plan judiciously so that extra space for banks of breeding cages can be left for the time when they will be needed, or an extra flight will be built on. Taking time to make plans, asking for advice from other fanciers and visiting other birdrooms pays dividends at this time.

The outside of the wooden building needs to be treated with a *nontoxic preservative* before any additional building is carried out.

An extra coat at this time can do no harm and may save a deal of maintenance in the future. For your own comfort and that of the birds, and for long-term savings on heating, the interior of the birdroom should be insulated, including the roof. *Polystyrene* is not recommended for this purpose because mice could get into it and use it for nesting purposes. *Fiberglass* or *rock wool* makes life far too uncomfortable for rodents to want to make nests.

If openings are needed into the flights, these should be cut out before the shed is lined. Small bob-holes may be useful in winter to prevent drafts, but in hot months it is better to have as much ventilation as possible. (See *VENTILATION*.) The ideal solution is to cut holes 46 × 46 cm (18 × 18 in) and then keep them partially blocked during the winter.

Before you line the birdroom, all electrical wiring should be installed so that no cables are available for the birds to nibble. Now line the shed with a good-quality 10 mm (⅜ in) plywood, laminated coated board, or other suitable material. All joints should be sealed with good-quality thick adhesive, so that should *mites* ever become a problem, there would be no cracks and crevices for them to escape from disinfectants and sprays. A coat of white or light-colored emulsion over the lining of the birdroom will lighten the whole building. At this point, wooden frames should be built in, onto which breeding cages will later be built.

Cages are the next priority. In a small birdroom the same cages can be used for breeding cages, stock cages, show preparation and even for internal flights. Using a 5 × 2.5 cm (2 × 1 in) piece of lumber, cut and screw this along the wall, then across the front. Next, panel in the floors/ceilings using plywood, with a piece of 5 × 2.5 cm lumber, running from front to rear beneath the cage floor levels. The fronts of the cages can be produced in single units or as a block. Using 5 × 2.5 cm lumber for all the uprights and 13 × 2.5 cm (5 × 1 in) for the

Winning champions

Normal grey green
cock.

Opaline grey green cock displaying the short, wide neck called for by the standard of excellence.

Normal light green cock.

A Capern's card showing a skyblue budgerigar.

Normal skyblue cock.

vertical pieces will produce a frame which can be attached to the floors/ceilings to form a block of cages. A coat of white emulsion on the new wood both protects and enhances its appearance.

Wire cage fronts can be purchased from a number of suppliers who advertise in the birdworld press. The fronts have wires trimmed off flush at the top and bottom of the cross wires, but a few of the wires are left longer for attachment to the wooden frames. Place the wire front against the frame and mark the places where the extended wires will be fixed, then drill a tiny hole, 2.5 cm (1 in) deep, in the center of the front rail of the cage. Place the wires of the front into the drilled holes and press home, then repeat at the top of the cage. It is necessary to bend the wire cage front slightly to allow it to spring into position where it will now be perfectly secure.

Removable slides are now fitted between each cage. These can be made of plywood, sheet metal, hardboard, plexiglass, glass or wire attached to a wooden frame. Wire has the disadvantage of allowing the birds to squabble and pull out each other's feathers, or to perch on the wire sides of their cages,

more interested in the occupants of the adjoining cages than in their own mates. Plywood, sheet metal and hardboard have the disadvantage of opacity, and therefore slides of glass or plexiglass are recommended. These give ease of cleaning and allow the birds to see the display and mating of their neighbors, which acts as a stimulus.

When fixing the door to your birdroom you cannot be too *security* minded. It should be as substantial as possible. If using a padlock, it is worthwhile buying one made from toughened steel, with a good locking mechanism. Ensure that the hasp and staple are bolted to the frame with the heads protected. *Never* fit the hinges of the door on the outside; it is far too easy for someone to take out the screws or knock out the pins. The safest fastening for your outside door is a good-quality mortise lock. Develop good habits in security. Never leave the key in the door, and once the birdroom is locked, keep the key in a safe place inside your house.

If there is space for a separate, but attached, storeroom, this is ideal. If not, try to keep as much equipment as possible off the floor so that if, by some unfortunate

A. Frame for inside flights

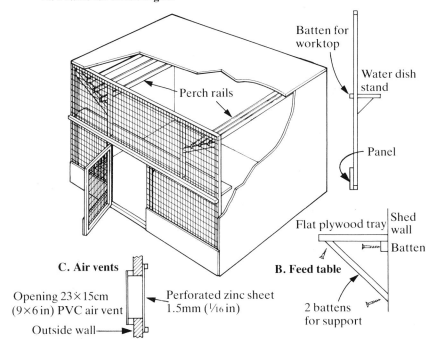

Batten for worktop

Water dish stand

Perch rails

Panel

Flat plywood tray

Shed wall

Batten

C. Air vents

Opening 23×15cm (9×6 in) PVC air vent

Perforated zinc sheet 1.5mm (1/16 in)

Outside wall

B. Feed table

2 battens for support

chance, mice should get into the birdroom, this will be spotted very quickly. Try to keep items in constant use in cupboards and avoid using cardboard containers because these become dust traps.

FLIGHTS, both inside and outside, are now necessary, and *HEATING* and *LIGHTING* need to be considered. They will be found under their own entries.

BOARD OF DIRECTORS
The Board of Directors is the governing body of the American Budgerigar Society. The executive committee consists of the president, first, second and third vice-presidents, treasurer, secretary and immediate past president. Officers are elected for a period of four years, after which they must seek re-election. The full board consists of the executive committee members plus the eleven district directors who are chosen by ballot. The board formulates the rules under which shows are set up, rules for judges and rules to ensure that the members always act in the best interests of the society. They set the standards of excellence and the scale of points, and generally manage the affairs of the ABS. District directors are elected for a period of four years. They arrange for annual district meetings to be held in each of the eleven districts each year.

The full Board of Directors meets whenever this is felt to be necessary by the executive committee, but always at least once a year. An AGM of all members is held annually at the All American where so many of the members congregate.

BREEDERS' AWARDS
In most shows, awards are given for breeder, or current-year banded birds. To qualify for these, the bird must be wearing the closed, coded band of the exhibitor, for the current year. It is always considered a greater achievement to win prizes with birds one has bred oneself, therefore breeders' awards are more highly prized than those for any age birds. This is recognized by donors of cups and trophies, who often stipulate that they should be given in the breeder section, and this stimulates the competition.

BREEDING CAGES
Basically there are two types of breeding cages in popular use. The *all-wire* cage is used widely in the United States and is gaining in

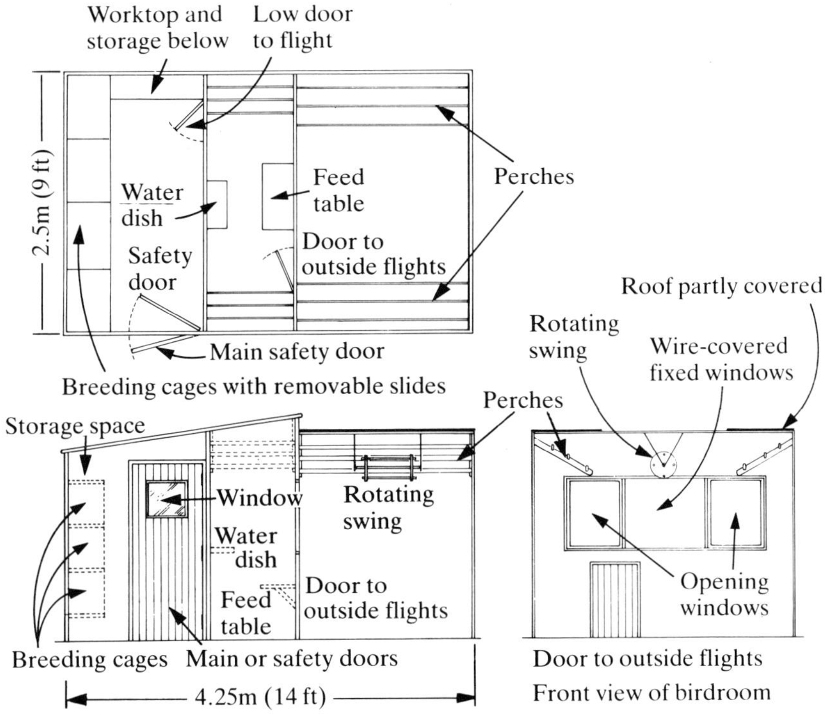

Diagram of a birdroom and flights.

Worktop and storage below — Low door to flight

2.5m (9 ft)

Water dish
Safety door
Feed table
Door to outside flights
Perches
Main safety door

Breeding cages with removable slides

Storage space
Window
Water dish
Feed table
Rotating swing
Door to outside flights
Perches
Breeding cages   Main or safety doors

4.25m (14 ft)

Roof partly covered
Rotating swing
Wire-covered fixed windows
Opening windows
Door to outside flights
Front view of birdroom

The opaline variety

A Capern's card showing an opaline light green cock.

Opaline light green cock with excellent opalescent wing markings.

Opaline dark green cock with wing markings showing an excess of body color.

Opaline cobalt cock.

A typical breeding cage.

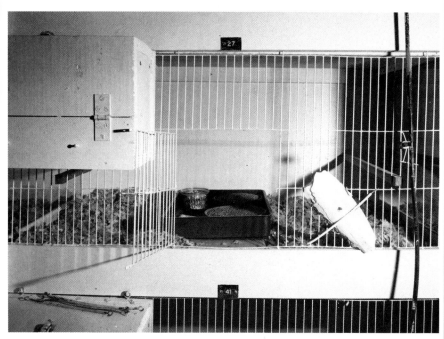

popularity in the UK. It consists of a six-sided box made from flat panels of rectangular welded wire mesh. Sizes vary, but the average size is 76 cm wide × 61 cm high × 61 cm deep (30 × 24 × 24 in). All the edges are clipped together with special wire clips to ensure the rigidity and security of the cage. A door is cut out in the front, secured at one side with clips, and a door fastener is fixed to the other side. Two perches are fitted at about the halfway mark and the cage hung onto hooks fitted to the wall. A small gap is left between the bottom of one cage and the top of the one below and a sheet of paper inserted to catch the droppings. It is unhygienic and dangerous to allow droppings from one cage to fall into another, as disease or parasites can be spread very easily in this way. One drawback of this type of cage is that if a chick came out of the nest too early, as they often do, there would be no dry litter in which it could keep warm if the weather was particularly cold.

The conventional type of breeding cage, used by the vast majority of breeders, is virtually a wooden box with a wire front. The needs and comfort of the birds should be of prime concern, even if it means cutting down on the number of cages the breeder would like to have, and the *minimum* size recommended is 76 cm wide × 46 cm high × 46 cm deep (30 × 18 × 18 in). A board placed across the bottom front prevents husks and other debris from falling to the floor. The best position for the large access door is in the center, as this enables the breeder to catch the birds more easily when necessary. From the point of view of cleanliness and attractiveness, it is recommended that the inside of the cage be painted with white or pale-colored emulsion paint. Nest boxes can be placed inside the cage or hung on the outside. If they are used on the outside, it is necessary to remove a small part of the wire to allow the birds access, and a small removable door should be fixed to close the opening in the wire front when the cage is not being used for breeding. Two perches are then fixed, preferably of 1.9 × 1.5 cm (¾ × ⅝ in) lumber.

Cages are normally ranged in banks, with removable side panels, which allows them to be used as stock cages for weaning the youngsters, for steadying birds prior to the show season and for show preparation. The sliding panels can be made from sheet metal, plywood, hardboard, stiff wire netting (though this could allow some squabbling between the pairs), glass or plexiglass. The latter two are favored because they allow more light into the cages and allow the birds to see each other, a seeming advantage during the breeding season.

At one time, trays were fitted to the base of breeding cages to facilitate cleaning and changing and replenishing food containers, but they are seldom used now.

BREEDING SEASON

The most important time of the year is the breeding season. On this depends the success or failure you will achieve on the show bench in the coming season. When it should begin is a subject of much controversy, but if you are breeding birds for exhibition, and provided that you have provision for artificial lighting and heating in your birdroom, then late November is the most convenient time for pairing up the birds. This means that the first chicks will be emerging at the end of the year, ready for the new issue of bands on January 1. Youngsters who are born early in the year have the opportunity to develop before the show season begins, and second-round chicks will also be independent by then, allowing you to clear and clean the birdroom before using some of the cages to house the show team.

Once you have selected your pair (see *PAIRING*), record the details of the color, sex and band number of both birds on the record card for that cage, put in the birds and leave them alone for two or three days to become acclimatized to their new surroundings. While you carry on filling the remainder of your breeding cages, or until all the birds with which you are satisfied have been paired up, watch to see there is no fighting between cock and hen. They must be happy together for satisfactory results. Three days later the nest boxes can be attached to the breeding cages and the pairs allowed to enter them at will. In ten to fourteen days' time, the hens should begin to lay eggs. Just before laying commences, the droppings of the hen become enlarged, far more copious and wetter than at other times of the year. Eggs are then laid on alternate days and each chick normally hatches on the eighteenth day after the egg is laid.

During the *incubation period* the egg requires heat which the hen is able to provide if left in peace. Hens can be upset, and even leave their eggs, if they are constantly disturbed by the anxious breeder opening the nest box for innumerable checks. A wise thing to remember is that the breeding cage is the budgies' home — you are the intruder.

Establish a routine to build up the birds' confidence. Visit the birdroom twice a day, preferably at the same time each day. Carry out your inspection and feeding in a regular order. For example, begin at the entrance and work towards the exit, or vice versa, but always in the same order. By checking through one cage at a time, you will never miss any bird which appears distressed in any way. One important thing to remember while checking the nest boxes is that by *handling* the eggs, you can never make an infertile egg fertile, but *you can be the cause of a fertile egg failing to hatch*. One rule you must follow is never to handle eggs or chicks with cold hands; either warm them on a radiator, keep a bowl of hot water available, or even take a hot water bottle with you to make sure that your hands are kept warm. During nest box inspection, any chicks old enough and big enough should be banded. (See *BANDING A CHICK*.)

The next task is to replenish the seed pots; then, soaked oats, greens or any other additives are distributed; and, finally, the water containers are refilled. It is worth remembering that the hen is in a very warm environment in the nest box. If she were to emerge and drink newly supplied, icy-cold water, it could cause troubles. To avoid this it is wise to fill a bucket of water and leave it overnight so that it will have reached room temperature by the time it is used.

It is unhygienic to leave the heavy droppings from the hens in

The cinnamons

Cinnamon light green cock.

Two Capern's cards showing cinnamon cobalt and cinnamon dark green budgerigars.

Cinnamon cobalt cock which shows clearly how the cinnamon factor dilutes the body color.

Cinnamon skyblue
cock.

the breeding cages. They can become moldy and are a breeding ground for bacteria. They should be removed at least twice a week.

Finally, and every time, remember to sweep the floor and leave the birdroom tidy.

Unfortunately, the breeding season brings its problems. The nest box should be checked each day once chicks have arrived. If the hen is a "dirty feeder" and manages to leave food around the face of the chick, this needs gently cleaning off with a piece of soft cloth and warm water, but be very careful as the chick is very weak when tiny and it would be easy to drown it with a very small amount of water. Be sure that no food is stuck inside the beak. If there is, it can be cleaned away, very gently, with a toothpick or matchstick. If it will not come off easily, it can be soaked off with a tiny amount of warm water.

Droppings do become stuck to the leg band as the youngsters grow. This is not a major problem, as the dirt can be cracked free when the chick is about four to five weeks old, by using your thumbnail. Again, if it cannot be cleaned by this method, soaking in warm water will remove it.

If the chick's feet become fouled with droppings, it is a more serious matter and requires attention to prevent the feet becoming malformed. Wash the feet with warm water until all the dirt is cleaned away, dry gently with a clean cloth and, to prevent any recurrence of the problem, remove any wet droppings from the nest box and replace with clean, dry sawdust.

When checking the nest boxes, it is necessary to note whether all the chicks are being fed. Sometimes, for no apparent reason, the parents stop feeding one particular baby. Whether they have taken a dislike to it, or whether it does not call for food as loudly as the others in the nest cannot be decided. There are occasions when a hen decides she will stop feeding a chick at a certain age, although she will continue to feed her younger offspring until they, too, reach the cutoff age. Unless action is taken, they will all die. In cases such as these, the chicks must either be transferred to another box and a foster mother, or be hand-fed, which is tedious and time-consuming. Wherever possible, the chicks should be transferred into a box where there are youngsters of a similar age. If left too long with parents who are not feeding, the chick will become too weak to call for food and will die. The chicks are accepted better if, before being put into the new box, they are rubbed with a little of the sawdust from the new box and the breeder holds them and any other chicks from the new box together, so that they will all share the same smell.

Occasionally a chick with a very *distended crop* is discovered. This is thought to be caused through poor feeding by the hen, but it could be that food has fermented and caused the crop to blow up like a balloon, or the cause might be that the nostrils have become jammed up with food and the baby has not realized it can also breathe through its mouth. Whatever the cause, prompt action is necessary if the chick is going to survive. First the nostrils should be examined, and if caked with food, this should be wiped off gently with a warm damp cloth, until they are free. Now the wind in the crop must be removed. The crop is pressed gently but firmly in an upwards direction and wind, sometimes together with a small amount of liquid, is expelled through the beak. These chicks will need watching more than others who appear to be well fed, because if the fault is incorrect feeding by the hen, wind may need to be expelled physically several times. Eventually the hen, usually a maiden, succeeds in feeding properly and no more gas is formed. If it is found that the condition persists for more than a few days and it is constantly necessary to "wind" the chick, it should be fostered to a good feeder. Sometimes it is a good plan to put a well-fed baby of the same age in with the hen who has been feeding badly, as such a baby seems able to teach the mother how to do the job properly, strange though it may seem.

Feather plucking is a problem which occasionally occurs. Some hens just pull out the fluffy down, but never touch the feathers. This can be ignored. Sometimes however, the plucking can be far more serious, ranging from a few feathers at the back of the chick's head, through stripping the back and wings, to a situation where the chick is so viciously attacked that it is killed. Careful observation is called for to identify whether the hen or cock is the culprit and when one is certain, that bird should be removed from the breeding cage and the other partner left to bring up the youngsters. The youngster which has been damaged should have some soothing ointment smeared onto the broken area of skin. If it is only a matter of a few feathers having been pulled out and the skin is left unbroken, that chick, and any others in the nest, can be sprayed with one of the proprietary anti-pecking liquids, or even with a strong-smelling perfume. Whichever is used, it is necessary to protect the chick's eyes while it is being applied.

Occasionally, an adventurous baby leaves the nest before it is fully feathered and before it is strong enough to withstand the environment outside the box. If, when found, it is chilled, do not place it straight back with the other chicks, but warm it first.

Sometimes the chicks are harassed by the cock once they have left the nest. There are several theories as to the reason for this. Sometimes the cock is trying to mate with his own baby daughters; sometimes the chicks interfere when the cock is trying to feed or mate with the hen; sometimes the chicks seem to worry at the cock to feed them continually. Whatever the cause, the cock may attack the youngster. It may only pull out flight feathers as the chick struggles to free itself from its bad-tempered father, but at other times the attack may be vicious and can end in the death of the chick. To avoid these problems, place a small box in a corner of the breeding cage, where the chicks can gather together in the same way as they did in the nest box. It is surprising how quickly this restores harmony and allows the chicks to remain safe and well fed.

A risky period is the time when the chicks are ready to be taken away from the parents. Make certain that they are more than 42 days old and observe that they are eating seed independently. Usually they will adapt to living with the other youngsters you have taken away without difficulty. On rare occasions, one chick is found which is not eating. If this is noticed within 48 hours of its being taken away, you can try putting it back in the cage with its parents, but you will need to sit somewhere away from the cage and watch for at least half an hour to ensure that neither parent attacks it. Provided the cock starts feeding the youngster, it is worth disturbing the hen to ensure that she has seen and accepted it before you leave the birdroom. Sometimes it is possible to persuade a pair with other chicks due to leave them shortly to accept the hungry chick, but never try this if the nest box is still up and until you have observed the reaction of the proposed foster parents.

Another problem which can occur in the nest box is a hen which sits too heavily on the chick, causing the legs to splay out and the body to lie flat. Unless this is corrected soon after it first happens, it can result in permanent distortion of the legs, to such an extent that the youngster will be unable to perch or walk and will have to be destroyed. As soon as a chick with *splayed legs* is discovered, it should be treated by putting a split band on the second leg and tying the two bands together with wool or soft string. The chick will be unable to walk properly and may appear distressed for a short time, but it will soon adapt to the new situation. The bands should be kept tied fairly tightly for ten days before the wool and split band are removed. By this time, the soft little legs will have hardened to a degree and will be growing straight again.

BUFF

The term buff is given to coarse- and loose-feathered birds. Under a low-powered microscope or a magnifying glass, it can be seen that these feathers are longer than normal and have tiny "hooks" on the ends. The bird also grows a thick layer of down, so that it appears larger than birds with smooth feathers (generally called "yellows"), but it has also been found more difficult to breed with. Although highly prized for the show bench, a buff bird should not be paired with another buff, to avoid production of double buffs, which could eventually lead to infertile stock.

BUYING BUDGERIGARS

Newcomers to budgerigar breeding may find the purchase of their first stock a difficult matter. When? Where? How much? They are beset with queries. The best time for buying stock is July and August. It is then that experienced fanciers are sorting out their year's stock and deciding which birds they can afford to dispose of and which they intend to keep. From the birds' point of view, it allows them to settle down into their new surroundings; in the autumn they will be able to molt in the environment in which they will be breeding and they will get used to the new water supply and to the methods of husbandry of their new owner. The newcomer is advised to purchase stock from an established breeder in his or her area, to whom he or she can then go back for advice should he or she run into any difficulties. If possible the first stock should be made up of six cocks and eight or nine hens. This will give the new breeder the chance of breeding from several pairs at the same time and allows for possible difficulties with some of the hens. Color should not be important in these early stages, but very often the newcomer has already adopted a preference for a particular color before beginning. A very simple rule to follow,

before the new breeder has a better understanding of genetics, is that if he or she starts with blue birds and then introduces one or more green, eventually green will take over as the dominant color. In the same way, if he starts with green and introduces grey, then grey will be the predominant color in a short while. If opaline markings are introduced into a breeding room along with normals, opaline will become predominant, and if cinnamons are then introduced, they will "take over."

What should you pay for your first birds? If breeding for exhibition is your goal, then you will need to start with birds of reasonable quality. Perhaps the best guide would be that the bird should cost about the same price as 25 kg (55 lb) of budgerigar seed. If pet breeding is your goal, then much lower-priced stock can be used. In this case color is a consideration, as pet buyers prefer pretty colors. The *ideal age* for your first stock should be between six and ten months. Birds at that age will be fully molted out; you should be able to see their full potential; and you will not be buying old birds which might have vices for which you, as a raw beginner, would not be prepared.

One thing which is not advised is for beginners to go out and pay "silly" prices for birds. Some beginners come into the fancy and are told that Mr. X has the best birds in the country and that if they can buy from him, they too will reach the heights. They are led to believe that they can cut out years of hard work and time spent learning the trade by spending huge amounts on their initial stock. This is absolutely untrue. If they know nothing about breeding budgerigars, then they will learn just as much from breeding pets as they will from breeding from the most expensive birds in the country — and they will make as many mistakes.

C

CAGES

Cages for pets are sold in all sizes and shapes. The first rule when buying a cage is that a bird flies from side to side and not vertically. The longer the cage, the better for the bird, especially if it is to spend a great deal of time in it. Very high cylindrical cages, while they may add to the decor of your home, are unsatisfactory for budgerigars.

A useful accessory, which can be bought at the same time as the cage, is a cover for the base of the cage, which will catch any falling seed. Budgerigars, especially babies, love to scratch and scatter seed, and a base cover or tray can prevent a lot of vacuuming.

Show cages are a necessity for the potential exhibitor. These are small wooden boxes with wire fronts in which the bird can be transported to shows in safety and in which they must be shown. Newcomers should check standards for cages with their budgerigar society.

BREEDING CAGES are dealt with under a separate heading.

CATCHING

To catch birds in an aviary, a catching net is an essential piece of equipment. When buying your first net, you should note the length of the handle. Handles are usually 30 cm (12 in) long, but if you are particularly short, or if your birdroom or flights are particularly high, then it is best to buy a net with a 46 cm (18 in) handle. To catch a bird, stand facing the bird you require, wave the net underneath the perch on which it is sitting to make it fly towards you and, keeping your eye upon it, swing the net smoothly, rather like an overhand shot in tennis, capturing the bird quite safely.

A pet bird can be captured easily in darkness. First close the curtains, making sure that there is

A catching net.

no open fire, or that it is safely covered. Watch where the bird has landed; then ask someone to switch off the light suddenly, and you'll find that the bird, surprised by the dark, can be picked up with ease.

CHALLENGE CERTIFICATES

These certificates are awarded by the UK Budgerigar Society at shows to which they give their higher levels of patronage. At area society shows and at their own world championship shows, challenge certificates are awarded for both breeder and any age sections, while at championship shows both breeder and any age bird in each color must compete for the same certificate.

These challenge certificates are highly prized by exhibitors and convey a certain amount of prestige to the winning bird. The name of the exhibitor, the show at which it was awarded, the judge's signature and, most important, the band number of the bird are recorded upon the certificate. No challenge certificate can be awarded to a bird unless the exhibitor is a member of the Budgerigar Society and has nominated BS on the entry form, and unless the bird is wearing a closed coded band purchased through the Budgerigar Society.

At a show, the system through

which the bird is chosen for this award is that each color is judged throughout all the sections. The first prizewinner of each color is then placed before the judge, who selects the best of those prizewinners. That bird is awarded the place of best of color. The entry form is then consulted to ensure that the exhibitor is a member of the BS and has nominated accordingly. The bird is checked to ensure that it is banded, that the band is a BS band, that it has in no way been tampered with and that it is a current-year band if the bird has been entered in breeder classes. If all these details are in order, the bird is awarded the challenge certificate; if not it is awarded the best of color place, but the next-placed bird which complies with all the appropriate regulations is awarded the CC.

Challenge certificates are awarded for the following varieties:

Normal green series (excl. grey green)
Normal blue series
Grey
Grey green
Opaline green series (incl. opaline grey green)
Opaline blue series (incl. opaline grey)
Normal cinnamon or greywing
Opaline cinnamon or opaline greywing green series
Opaline cinnamon or opaline greywing blue series
Lutino
Albino
Whitewing
Yellowwing
Dominant pied or clearflight
Recessive pied or dark-eyed clear
Crest or tuft
Yellowface (excl. yellowface pieds)
Any other color not otherwise competing for a certificate

CHAMPION
This is the highest status for exhibitors. It is the section from which most of the top award winners come, because before an exhibitor reaches this status, he or she has usually spent many years of dedicated hard work. To become a

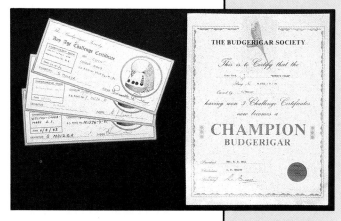

champion, the exhibitor must first have advanced through the novice and intermediate divisions. As an intermediate, he or she must have won any of the first through sixth best in show at three different shows and all the birds with which he or she won must have been of his or her own breeding and banded with his or her own bands. All the shows at which the wins were attained must have been open shows. Wins at any of the smaller shows, such as baby shows, parlor shows, invitational, or any show which restricts the entry, cannot be counted towards advancement.

Once an exhibitor has moved up to the champion division, he or she is not allowed to drop back.

In other countries the rules of status and advancement differ from those of the USA. Several countries, including the UK, allow exhibitors to choose to advance to a higher division if they wish, but most insist that once the exhibitors have achieved the requisite number of wins, they must advance and then they may not drop back.

CHAMPION BIRDS
In the UK a budgerigar can become a champion bird by winning three *challenge certificates*, at least one of which must be won in adult classes. Alternatively, it can win three *best of color certificates* in place of one or more of the challenge certificates. A budgerigar cannot become a champion bird exclusively in breeder classes. Once the necessary certificates have been accumulated, they are sent to the Budgerigar Society office for

A prized champion bird certificate with the three challenge certificates needed to obtain it.

verification and a *champion bird certificate* is then issued. It has become the custom for birds achieving this honor to be given names as well as their numbers.

CHICKWEED

No other type of greens seems to be more enjoyed by budgerigars than chickweed. The plant should be gathered when fresh, and care taken that it is not growing in a position where it could be fouled by gasoline fumes or animal excrement, or sprayed with weedkiller. Chickweed, like all other forms of greens, should not be gathered if it has been affected by frost. It should be washed and given to the birds while it is still wet, because they delight in rolling in it in this state. Any which is not eaten at the end of each day should be removed because it goes bad if left overnight and could cause diarrhea. (See also *GREENS*.)

CHLAMYDIA

This disease, also known as *psittacosis*, is rare in budgerigars, but it is also the only disease suffered by these birds which can be transmitted to people. It manifests itself as a chest and respiratory disease, usually with enteritis, slimy, green droppings and runny eyes in the birds. It is a serious disease, but it can be cured. In human beings, *Chlamydia psittaci* can cause anything from a mild cold to serious, prolonged, feverish chest disease, sore throats, respiratory distress, lethargy and severe headaches, and is also contagious. It can be very serious in small children. Breeders who suspect that any of their birds are suffering from chlamydia should contact an avian veterinarian immediately. Breeders who suspect that they or a member of their family could have contracted psittacosis should tell a doctor the circumstances immediately.

CHOOSING YOUR PET

Two things are vital when choosing your pet budgerigar. It must be healthy and it must be young. The eyes should be bright, it should stand alert, there should be no sign of green or wetness around the vent, there should be no watery discharge from the nose. To decide whether the budgie is young or not, refer to the entry under *AGE*. It cannot be stressed too strongly that the bird should be under four months old if it is to make the perfect pet which will learn to talk and become completely tame. Color is a matter of individual choice. There is a huge range from which to choose and most breeders, even if they do not themselves breed the variety or color you desire, can usually introduce you to someone else who does. It has often been said that cocks are more likely to talk than hens, but this is a fallacy. Budgies learn to talk by mimicry and the more they are spoken to, the more they learn to mimic. It is true, however, that cock birds usually have more friendly temperaments than hens, but provided one gains their confidence, hens can be very affectionate. Cocks have a blue *cere* (the band above the beak), while in the hen this is brown. However, as babies the cere is not fully developed and it is often difficult to distinguish between the two. It is advised that, where possible, the pet buyer who is not buying from an experienced breeder should be accompanied by one.

CHROMOSOMES

A chromosome is the nucleus of the cell, and the cell is the unit of life. In each cell in its body the budgerigar has thirteen pairs of large chromosomes and a number, which it has been impossible to ascertain, of smaller chromosomes. These carry the genes which determine the bird's color, size, size of spots, shape and every other characteristic. All the chromosomes appear in pairs except the sex chromosome. The cock has two of these, while the hen has only one X, or sex, chromosome and one smaller one which is designated as Y. This difference is very important and will be discussed in detail under *SEX LINKAGE*.

CINNAMON FACTOR

The cinnamon factor is one of the mutations which has appeared in budgerigars over the years. It is sex-linked, that is, it cannot be carried in a hidden form by the hen. The effect of this factor is to change all the black feathers into cinnamon brown and to soften the main body color.

CLASSIFICATION

It is important for breeders to read the classification in show catalogs because this can differ from show to show. The ABS does not dictate to its affiliates how their classification is to be set up. In an area where they are strong in certain rare varieties, they will arrange more sections to accomodate them; where there are only a few rare breeders then all the classes will be lumped together under "rare varieties." In the US, 90 percent of shows call for exhibits to be bred and banded by the exhibitor, and care must be taken to make sure that bought birds are not entered in these classes. A few shows do have what is called an open division, but normally the winner of this division cannot be considered for the best in show awards. In almost every case there are separate classes scheduled for *old* and *young* birds. These must be observed carefully, as at most shows it is an offense to enter old birds in the young classes, or to enter a bird in young classes which is not wearing the closed coded band of the exhibitor. It is also important to check that the *class number* used from the classification is for the correct status under which the breeder wishes to show, because once he or she has exhibited under a higher status, it is not possible to revert to a lower one unless there are no classes scheduled for his or her status (in this case it is allowable to show in the next higher status without affecting future shows). For example, if the schedule shows only intermediate classes, it is permissible for a novice to enter in intermediate classes for that show and then to revert to his own status at any later shows. Young classes are sometimes referred to as current-year classes. In some countries no bird may be shown in any class unless it was bred by the owner.

CLEARFLIGHT

A mutation which appears to be related to the *pied variety*, the clearflight, as its name implies, has visible flight feathers of clear yellow or white on its wings, according to the basic color. The correct number for show purposes is seven. It also has a small patch of clear color at the back of the head.

CLEARWINGS

First bred in 1933 in Australia, this mutation of budgerigars was much sought after when they were introduced into the UK a year later. However, when it was found that they were much smaller than the normal variety and that, because they were recessive to normals, it was difficult to improve the size, they became less popular with exhibitors. In good specimens the body color is enhanced from that of the normal varieties and the wings are of a clear color, lacking the *melanin markings*.

CLOSED CODED BANDS

These bands are supplied only by the American Budgerigar Society in the United States, by the BS in the United Kingdom and by the ruling body for the hobby in other countries. They are made from aluminum which has been dyed to a specific color. The color changes each year. On the band is stamped the year, the individual code number of the breeder and then the serial number of the band, for example, 87 (year), M1574 (code

Closed coded bands.

number), 107 (serial number). The bands are placed on the legs of the chicks at between five and ten days of age. Once the bones have hardened, it is impossible to remove the bands except by cutting them off.

CLUTCH

A number of eggs laid by the hen of a breeding pair is called the clutch. In the wild, in Australia, a clutch of eggs is usually four, all of which hatch. In captivity the number ranges on average from three to nine and, unfortunately, a number fail to hatch. Some are *clear* or *infertile*. Others die before they have started to form into chicks and are said to be *addled*. Others begin to form into baby budgerigars and then die along the way; these are designated *dead in shell*. And then there are those which develop right up until the time of hatching, but lack the strength to break out of their shells.

The eggs are laid every other day and hatch in the same order, so that in a large clutch which all hatch successfully, it is possible to have one chick just a day old while the oldest is two weeks old. This causes problems with the big brother trampling all over the tiny baby, and the hen having run out of crop milk by the time the youngest is born. To prevent this situation, the older chicks are usually transferred to a nest containing chicks of roughly the same age, leaving the mother to bring up the smaller babies.

COD LIVER OIL

Cod liver oil emulsion is widely used to mix with canary seed during the breeding season. Some people feel that this could be the cause of *French molt*, but none of the research into the disease has served to confirm this belief. Experience has shown that the addition of a *small* amount of emulsion is beneficial to breeding hens and prevents *egg binding*, but this should not be given in excess. The amount recommended is one tablespoon to a 9 liter (2 gal) bucket of canary seed, well mixed

This clutch of eggs indicates the variation in size and shape that is possible in budgerigar eggs.

in. Emulsion is preferable to plain oil, as it keeps better. Only enough for a week's supply should be mixed at a time, and in hot climates smaller amounts should be mixed, to ensure that the oil is never allowed to become rancid.

COLONY SYSTEM

The colony system of breeding is not one to be recommended. The theory is to keep an even number of cocks and hens together and then supply them with far more nest boxes than there are pairs. Even when this precaution is taken, there are often fights among the hens for one particular nest box and these can be quite serious; in fact, hens have been known to fight to the death. If the reader should wish to follow this system, then the nest boxes should be positioned high up, near the roof, and should not be supplied until the weather has become warm in spring. Always supply at least a third more nest boxes than there are pairs. Within a week you should see pairs going in and out of the nest boxes, around 18 to 21 days later the chicks should be hatching, and after a further 30 to 40 days the youngsters should be flying around the flight. Remember that certain colors are dominant and if you start with some greens among the flock, then eventually green will take over. The same thing happens with greys. They are a dominant variety and soon there will be more and more greys and grey greens and fewer and fewer blues.

Also remember that when colony breeding is practiced, the aviary can soon become overcrowded with birds, and unless all nest boxes are removed, the birds will keep on breeding, with chicks starting to hatch every ten weeks. Be sure to remove *all* the nest boxes once the chicks have started to fly; this prevents quarrelling among the hens.

COLORS

The range of colors and varieties of budgerigars becomes a source of amazement for the uninitiated. From the first wild normal light greens have mutated and evolved yellows, blues, pieds, clearwings, spangles, lutinos and a range which gives a wide choice to those seeking a pet or a variety upon which to concentrate when breeding.

COLOR STANDARDS

These standards are set by the American Budgerigar Society in the US and the Budgerigar Society in the UK. They vary little from country to country. They consist of a minutely detailed description of the correct color of wings, cheek patches, eyes, tail, etc., of all the colors and varieties. The ABS recognizes the opaline form of clearwings and accepts that spangles may have black markings on the spots, but in all other respects uses the color standards of the BS. A publication giving full details of the American standards of perfection can be obtained from the ABS for a few dollars.

CONDITION

Condition is a term used to describe fitness for a desired goal. A budgerigar is in *show condition* when it has its complete set of feathers and those feathers are well groomed and have a bloom of good health. The eye is bright, the stance is upright, the vent is clean and the bird alert. It is in *breeding condition* when it has no sign of illness (wet or stained vent, discharge from eyes or nose, breathing difficulties, etc.), is alert and active, is tapping at the perches and, if housed together, is

paying a great deal of attention to the opposite sex. It's not necessary for the birds' feathers to be perfect for them to be in breeding condition.

CONDITION SEED

This is a mixture of seeds which acts as a tonic to the birds and is generally greatly enjoyed. It is usually purchased ready-mixed from a seed merchant. Condition seed should only be given as an extra and rationed accordingly, otherwise some birds might try to live exclusively on their favorite seeds which can have unfortunate results, particularly as one food which is often a favorite is hemp seed, which has an intoxicating effect.

CREST

All colors of budgerigars can be shown under the crest classification. Crests are distinguished by a number of feathers on the head growing in a different direction from the others, causing one of the three types of crests to appear. The *plain crest*, or *tuft*, consists of just a few feathers standing more or less upright in the center of the head; the *half-circular crest* is a semicircle of feathers rising or falling in a fringe just above the cere; the *full-circular crest* is flat, with the feathers radiating from the center and falling all around the head in a circular fringe.

CUTTLEFISH

Cuttlefish bone, which is readily available from seed merchants and pet stores, is a vital source of calcium for the birds. It is beneficial to make it available at all times of the year, but during the breeding season it is absolutely essential, so that the hens are provided with a source of calcium from which to lay down supplies in the shell gland for the shells of their eggs.

D

DARK FACTOR
The addition of two dark factors to the basic colors has led to some confusion in the names of the colors. A green bird carrying two dark factors is called an olive green, while if it carries only one dark factor it is referred to as a dark green. Similarly, with the blue colors, one dark factor results in a cobalt bird and two dark factors produce a mauve.

DEAD IN SHELL
When a chick is termed dead in shell, it means that it has developed for ten days or more and then, for some reason, died before it was hatched. Sometimes the reasons for this can be discovered by the fancier. It could be that the hen was uncomfortable and spent long periods away from the nest box. Perhaps the cock was disturbing the hen, or not supplying sufficient food and she came off the eggs to feed — and stayed away too long. In many instances the breeder is to blame, by continually disturbing the hen when looking in the nest box or showing the eggs to visitors to the birdroom. Infection can be another cause. Bacteria can be introduced from the hands of the breeder, or from droppings in the nest box, and can permeate the porous shell of the egg to infect the chick inside.

In some cases, the chick remains alive until it actually begins to chip its way out of the shell and then dies before it is clear. Sometimes this is a case of the chick being too weak to achieve its freedom from the confines of the egg, and in this case it would probably not survive into adulthood even if it were assisted, but in some instances the inside membrane of the shell has become overdry and tough and in this case the hen may help by prising apart the two halves of the shell herself. Breeders may wish to attempt this themselves, but must be very careful not to injure the tiny chick.

DIET
The basic diet of the budgerigar is canary and millet seed, with the addition of essential vitamins and minerals. The subject is dealt with fully under *FEEDING*.

DISEASES see *AILMENTS AND DISEASES*

DISINFECTANTS
It has been said that the finest disinfectant of all is strong bright sunlight after all debris has been removed by plenty of hot soap and water. However, as we cannot rely on strong sunlight just when we need it, and certainly cannot bring it inside our birdrooms, we need to use something really strong with which to remove all traces of bacteria or mite. The strongest, and most effective, disinfectant is one which is chlorous-based but, unfortunately, this is not one of the safest and if it is used where birds will have access to the surfaces treated, it should be well rinsed off with water. The simplest chlorous-based disinfectant is old-fashioned washing soda (sal soda), but there are many proprietary brands on the market. One of the safest disinfectants for use on utensils and surfaces to which the birds have access is one with an iodine base, such as Vanodine, or some other suitable preparation recommended by your veterinarian.

At the end of the breeding season, all the wire netting in the inside and outside flights should be washed down with a strong solution of iodine-based disinfectant and allowed to dry before the birds are reintroduced. All food and water containers must be removed before any disinfectants are used. The floor and walls of the outside flights should be really soaked with a strong chlorous-based disinfectant and later sprayed to rinse off any residue. Nest boxes and perches should be removed from the breeding cages, the fronts taken off, and emptied of whatever litter is used, scraped, brushed and then scrubbed with the iodine-based solution. Finally, the nest boxes, their blocks and the perches are scraped, brushed and soaked in a strong solution of disinfectant, liquid soap and paraffin. They are then scrubbed well and left in the sun to dry. Before they are stored away for the next season, a sprinkling of carbolic powder inside will ensure that they are kept mite-, lice- and bacteria-free. Before the cage fronts are put back, any necessary painting should be done and the cages sprayed with an anti-mite spray or water containing a solution of mite killer and repellent to prevent future infestation.

The most important thing to remember when carrying out the disinfection of your birdroom is that no food or water should have been left in a position where it could be contaminated by the disinfectants being used, and that the birds are removed from whichever part of the aviary you are cleaning in order to prevent them from inhaling harmful fumes or touching harsh cleaning substances.

DOMINANT FACTOR
Certain factors are dominant to others, which means that if you introduce these into your stock and breed indiscriminately, the factor which is dominant will eventually take over. Grey is a dominant factor and is visible in the green series as a modifying agent which changes the color of green to grey green; in the blue series it masks the blue color completely and results in an all grey bird. Other dominant factors are the green series, the Australian pied and violet, with a possibility of the spangle variety also being dominant, although this is, as yet, not conclusively established.

DRAFTS
Human beings find drafts uncomfortable, but for a budgerigar they are fatal. Although they can withstand cold, will play in the snow and seem to enjoy flying around in windy weather, they cannot tolerate drafts. They will sit in a draft without moving away and very quickly become ill. When building a birdroom it is very important to ensure that the perches are fixed so that no drafts can occur in that area. With a little thought, good ventilation can be achieved without the birds having to suffer drafts.

Another way that birds can be placed in a drafty position is in traveling to or from a show. Car windows may be left slightly open, or the car ventilation system left on, with a cage near one of the outlets. Care should be taken to ensure that this does not happen, or a light cover placed over the show cages so that no drafts can enter. Covering the cages being transported to a show also has the advantage of keeping out flashing lights from passing cars or from street lighting which could disturb or frighten the birds.

A pet cage should never be hung where it might be in a draft from an open window or door. Again, if open doors or windows are necessary, the cage should be protected by a cloth cover thrown over the side open to the draft. This should be held securely with clothespins or something similar to make sure that the playful budgie does not push it away from inside the cage.

Drafts, of course, are not the same as plain fresh air. Budgerigars benefit greatly from clean fresh air and sunshine.

DRINKERS
For pet cages, the most sensible drinker is the fountain type. It clips onto the cage, the level of water is always visible, and the bird cannot splash the water around or try to use it as a bath. For birdrooms and aviaries, various types are described under *WATER*. (See also *AUTOMATIC WATERING SYSTEM*.)

DUAL MEMBERSHIP
Two adults, being members of the same family and living in the same household, may become dual members of the ABS and pay dues

of 133⅓% of the regular dues. They do, however, lose certain rights by electing to be dual members. In the UK, a blood or marriage relationship to the other members of a partnership is not necessary. Partnerships are often a matter of convenience. One partner takes the birds to a show one week and the other the next, and each looks after the other's birds when he or she is on vacation. There is no restriction on the number of breeders who join together as a partnership. The Budgerigar Society (UK) subscription for partnerships is the same as if each person is a single member, and there are rules which must be followed. In the first year a partnership is formed, it may show birds in breeders' classes wearing any one of the partnership's band numbers, but in subsequent years one band number is normally allocated by the BS office, which all members of the partnership must use to allow them to exhibit their young stock.

Various types of drinkers. On the right is a fountain type of drinker which can be clipped onto a cage.

E

EGG BINDING

Lack of calcium can be one cause of egg binding. Sometimes the hen does not have sufficient supplies of this mineral to lay down around the yolk of the egg to make the shell, which results in the shell being malleable. The hen struggles to eject the egg which, being soft, elongates itself. This sort of straining can cause permanent damage to the hen and should be avoided at all costs. A supply of calcium must be always available. Oystershell and limestone grits are soluble forms of calcium, and cuttlefish, which is an integral part of the breeding cage furniture, is another valuable source.

Sometimes a hen has been put down to breed before being sufficiently mature and has trouble passing the egg through muscles which are not fully formed.

A diet containing plenty of greens (provided that greens have been given regularly in the past) and mixed seeds — with the canary seed treated with a small quantity of cod liver oil emulsion — is usually sufficient to prevent egg binding. Most causes of egg binding could and should be avoided.

If a hen does become egg bound, she should be moved, very gently to avoid breaking the egg inside her, to a show cage which can be placed before a hot fire or near a radiator. Before a bird in a cage is left in front of a radiator or an open fire, place a hand in front of the cage and leave it there to test the heat. Only when the heat is comfortable to the back of your hand should the cage be left unattended. It is unkind to leave a bird in a position where the heat is too great; it causes the bird great distress and it can soon become dehydrated. If a thermometer is available, the ideal temperature is 27° C (80° F). Now, with a feather

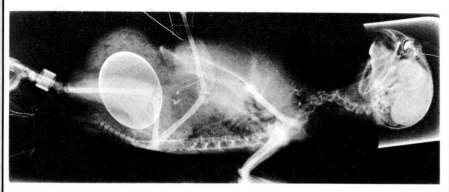

This x-ray shows a hen with a fully-formed egg about to be laid. Notice how large the egg is in proportion to the size of the bird.

or a very soft brush, the vent of the egg-bound hen should be coated with olive oil and she should be kept warm until she has expelled the egg.

EGG PRODUCTION
When the female *germ cell*, or *blastodisc*, falls into the *oviduct*, hopefully, a male *spermatazoa* will be waiting to fertilize it. A little further down the oviduct it is sheathed in *albumen*; even further along its journey, the membranes are formed and finally it reaches the *shell gland* where the hen has laid down stocks of calcium in readiness to make the shell. Once this is achieved, the egg is complete and after a short period needed for the egg to harden, it is laid.

EQUIPMENT
Much of the equipment used in a birdroom can be made at home. A very successful *food tray* can be made by using a length of PVC drainpipe with a table attached to the top. The table needs a 5 cm (2 in) surround to prevent food falling to the ground, where it could attract vermin. The use of a smooth section of pipe as a pedestal also prevents mice gaining access to the food. It is best to have glass or metal hoppers on the table to prevent fouling by the birds' droppings. Another base for the tray could be two plastic buckets.

Yet another feeding method is to make a box and place a rigid wire tray inside it about 5-7.5 cm (2-3 in) from the top. The seed dishes are then placed on the wire grid and all the husks, grit and debris fall into the box to be emptied out.

Always remember to place the feeding trays at a low level, because flying back upwards helps birds to develop muscles.

A perfect container for *soaking seed* can be made from two ordinary PVC buckets. A 7.5 liter (2 gal) bucket is drilled with several hundred tiny holes, around 3 mm (⅛ in) diameter. Oats or mung beans are placed in this and

it is then placed inside an 11 liter (3 gal) bucket filled with water. The contents of the smaller bucket can then be washed through with ease, and when the seed is ready to be given to the birds, all that is necessary is to lift out the smaller bucket and swing it around two or three times to remove all the excess water.

A *rotating swing* is very easy to make from four pieces of 5 × 2.5 cm (2 × 1 in) lumber. Make them into two Xs, and then take four pieces of 2 cm (¾ in) hardwood doweling and fix them between the

A bucket drilled with numerous holes to allow water to drain away into a larger bucket in which it stands. It is used to soak oats, mung beans and other food stuffs.

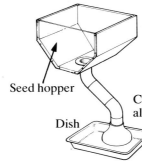

Box constructed of any rigid material with one side plexiglass to make seed content visible.

4cm (1½in) or 4.5cm (1¾in) flange fitting in base.

PVC waste fittings and pipe allow seed to flow into dish wherever it is positioned.

Seed hopper

Cut the top off a plastic bottle to allow the seed to spread.

Dish

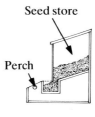

Seed store

Perch

Box mounted on sloping base feeds seed into tray by gravity.

Glass or plexiglass front shows seed level.

Husks are scattered by foraging birds.

two end crosses. Fix a screw at the center of each end and suspend the swing from the roof of the outside flight. (See page 134.)

One useful item of equipment, which cannot be made at home, is an *air cleaner*. These were made originally for cleaning the dust from calf houses, but are ideal for taking away the considerable amount of dust formed by the birds continually picking off minute pieces of their feather quills. The air cleaner works on the principle of sucking air into its interior, which is filled with electrically charged plates. Any dust in the air is deposited on these plates before the air is expelled again. It is necessary to take out the plates and wash them occasionally. The amount of dust collected is very considerable.

Another useful item is an *electronic insect exterminator*. This unit emits ultraviolet light, which attracts most species of flying insects. They fly into the bars and the moment they touch these they are incinerated. These exterminators are very efficient in keeping the birdroom free from flying creatures of all kinds, including moths, which seem to congregate in seed and nest boxes. The dead insects fall into a tray which is easily emptied. The unit is very cheap to run. A wire guard must be fitted over it to prevent a bird which has become loose from flying into it.

A *humidifier* and *humidistat* are used in many birdrooms although their efficacy is often challenged. Their advocates feel that a humidity of 15° C (60° F) is vital to the hatchability of eggs, but others feel that the humidity of the birdroom has little effect on the hatching rate of eggs and that this is controlled by the micro climate around the egg itself. Many things can affect the humidity underneath the hen. Some sawdusts have a drying effect; some of the peats, if used damp, can create a humidity which will cause the egg to drown the forming chick. All materials appear to have their advantages and disadvantages, but since the most popular nest materials are sawdust and wood shavings, it would appear that these are giving the best results.

In regard to very sophisticated equipment, an item which can prevent worry for breeders who are away from home during the day and are unable to visit their birds until the evening is a *photoelectric cell* fitted to the outside of the birdroom. If there is a thunderstorm or if for any other reason the light dips below a certain point, the main lights of the birdroom come on and the birds are undisturbed by the storm. When the light returns to a level above the cutoff point, the lights are turned off automatically.

The humble clothespin has so many uses. It can be used for

holding greens, millet sprays, cuttlefish, pet cage covers or nest box record cards, to name but a few items.

Another small item with a hundred uses is a "Pop-On." This is a clip made from wire springs, advertised in the birdworld press, which will fasten almost anything.

EXHIBITING

Exhibiting is the lifeblood of the budgerigar fancy. Although a few breeders are content to breed the little birds just for the love of their quaint antics and wonderful range of colors, the vast majority are drawn into the competitive world of bird shows, all certain that they have the dedication and knowledge necessary to reach the heights. At the outset, in the novice division, in their own small club, they start to win rosettes and awards. It is this which causes many to "get bitten by the budgie bug," as it is known in the fancy, and many years of competitive exhibiting, with the camaraderie, traveling and excitement which this entails, will follow. There are a number of rules to be complied with when exhibiting, which are given under separate headings.

EYES

A budgerigar's eyes should be bright and alert. If there is any sign of a discharge from the eyes, or if they are dull and lifeless, it is a sure sign that all is not well. The bird should be caged separately, kept warm and observed until the reason for its condition is discovered. Any proprietary eyewash for human use can be used to treat the eyes of birds which are red and sore after a seed husk has been caught beneath the lids, or after the bird has been in a draft. The budgerigar should be held on its side, and one or two drops of the eyewash should be dropped into the eye from an eyedropper, or squeezed from a piece of cotton wool soaked in the eyewash.

FALLOWS

The fallow factor dilutes the color of the normal budgerigar to a much paler shade. The English fallows have bright red eyes, without an iris ring, while the German fallows have eyes of a deeper red, with the typical white iris ring of the normals.

FANCY

The budgerigar fancy is the name given to the hobby of breeding and exhibiting budgerigars. The US parent body is the American Budgerigar Society which is divided into eleven districts. The district officers appointed to represent the districts on the Board of Directors of the ABS have the responsibility of administering and leading the hobby in their respective districts. They must make certain that the affiliated societies set up their shows in accordance with the rules formulated by the ruling body, and generally encourage the local societies affiliated with the ABS. On payment of annual dues, ready-formed clubs, or groups of seven or more budgerigar breeders, may become affiliates of the ABS.

District 1 consists of all New England and New York. District 2 takes in Kentucky, Ohio, West Virginia and Michigan. District 3 consists of Pennsylvania, Delaware, New Jersey, Maryland and District of Columbia. District 4 covers Indiana, Illinois and Wisconsin. District 5 administers Florida. District 6 is made up of Alabama, Tennessee, Mississippi, Louisiana and Arkansas. District 7 covers Minnesota, North and South Dakota, Missouri, Iowa, Nebraska and Kansas. District 8 has Texas, New Mexico, Colorado and Oklahoma to look after. District 9 is made up of Alaska, Washington, Oregon, Montana,

Wyoming, Idaho and counties of California including Kings, Monterey, Tulare, San Benito, Inyo and the area to the north of these counties. District 10 consists of Hawaii, Arizona, Nevada, Utah and counties of California including San Luis, Obispo, Kern, San Bernadino and the area to the south. District 11 takes in North and South Carolina, Georgia and Virginia.

The local clubs hold meetings where speakers share their knowledge, and also hold shows where novices can learn about the art of exhibiting. The newcomers very soon join the ABS, to enable them to obtain *closed coded bands*. Birds not wearing these bands can compete in very few shows, because in most shows the stipulation for entry is that the birds should have been bred and banded by the exhibitor. Every member of the ABS is allocated an exclusive band number which cannot be used by any other breeder in the world, so when one of that breeder's birds has been banded, it is identified for life.

The ABS holds a district meeting of members in each of its eleven districts every year, usually in conjunction with the district's annual regional show. Every member of the society receives a monthly magazine giving all the news of the society, together with articles on breeding and exhibiting budgerigars. Many US breeders also join the Budgerigar Society in the UK, in order to obtain the BS magazines which often carry color pictures of the various varieties. Enthusiasts of particular varieties are also likely to join the specialist societies for *clearwings*, *lutinos* and *albinos*, *crests*, *rare varieties* and *colors* and for *variegated* budgerigars, all of which are UK-based – their addresses appear under **USEFUL ADDRESSES**.

FAULTS
Judges discard or penalize birds showing any of the major faults. Some of these faults relate only to the variety being judged, such as *lutinos* showing a green suffusion,

or *albinos* showing blue; some relate to most of the varieties, for example, flecking of *melanin* on the top of the head, a tail which droops down at an angle, or crossed wing tips. The aim is to breed a bird as near as possible to the standard which is considered ideal by the ruling body for the country in which the show is being held. Most of the faults are uniform and worldwide.

FEATHERS
As far as the bird is concerned, the feathers perform three functions: they help it to fly, they help it to retain heat and they are a barrier against moisture. The serious

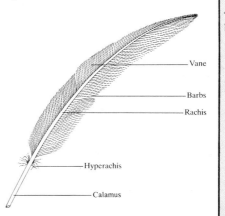

The structure of a budgerigar feather.

Vane

Barbs

Rachis

Hyperachis

Calamus

Feathers carrying spots of different shapes at different levels.

exhibitor studies the density of the feathers, their length and texture. The budgerigar with coarse or buff feathers will look larger than its fine or yellow-feathered companions. A spot carried on a short feather will give the impression of a narrow mask, while a spot of equal size on a long feather will appear much lower down the mask. The keen exhibitor will, however, have to take into consideration the fact that the long, coarse-feathered birds have proved less productive than their fine-feathered friends in the breeding cages.

Feathers can give an indication

of the health of the bird. On a very hot summer's day, the bird will fluff out its feathers to allow every bit of air to reach the skin and so cool it down, but if this condition is noticed on a cold day, it is a sure indication that the bird has a high temperature and is trying to lose heat. In this case it should be caught, caged separately, kept warm, and observed for any signs of illness, and appropriate action should be taken. If the feathers on top of the head or around the beak

A feather duster.

are matted, it is a sign that the bird has been vomiting, or that there is a discharge from the beak and nostrils. Again, this is something which must be investigated.

Budgerigars constantly *preen* their feathers to keep them in good condition and to "rainproof" them. They possess a preening gland at the base of the wings which produces a substance similar to lanolin with which they coat each feather. When the fancier sprays the bird's feathers regularly before a show, this removes a tiny amount of the lanolin and so encourages the bird to preen and keep its feathers in perfect order. If a bird is seen with lackluster, straggly feathers, it usually means that it is not preening, which indicates that the bird may be unwell. The usual routine of catching and observing is necessary.

FEATHER DUSTERS

These unfortunate birds have been called the "Down's syndrome" victims of the budgerigar world. During their early formation they appear the same as their normal brothers and sisters, but at the age of around four weeks, the growth of their feathers changes. There is more space between each follicle and the feathers begin to grow long and curled. Before long the chick appears to be much larger than its contemporaries, very often much larger than its parents. It continually loses the long feathers and then grows more of the same type. Most of its day is spent in searching for food and eating. Although not blind, it often seems unsure of where to find its food. If it is placed in the middle of a food dish it will eat ravenously, but soon lose its bearings and be found in another part of the cage. It is believed that the cause of this condition is hereditary, but no conclusive evidence of this has been found. The life span ranges from a few weeks to several months, but these birds seldom survive to adulthood.

FEATHER PLUCKING

Feather plucking is a most annoying habit and is difficult to stop. The hen is usually the culprit and often starts to pluck out the feathers of her babies simply out of the boredom of sitting in a nest box for a long period. It has been suggested that this habit is hereditary, or that a hen which has been plucked when she was a baby is likely to pluck her own chicks. If the hen simply pulls out the fine down and stops before the feathers begin to grow, little harm is done, but in some cases the hen will actually pull out the feathers, sometimes drawing blood and causing the youngster a great deal of distress. In severe cases, the feathers never regrow and the bird is useless for show purposes even provided that it recovers from the hen's attack. There are a number of proprietary liquids available to paint or spray onto the chick, which should deter the hen. Alternatively, the chick can be plastered with a greasy face cream or petroleum jelly to make it too unpalatable to pluck. If nothing stops the hen from plucking, she should be removed and the cŏck left to rear the chicks.

FEEDING

Budgerigars need protein, fats, carbohydrates, vitamins and minerals to keep them in good health, but at different times of the year these are required in different proportions. As well as the climatic seasons, it is necessary to take into account the molting season, the breeding season, the growing period of young birds and the show season.

During *the molt*, or *resting season*, feeding should be fairly basic. At this time of the year the birds are not very active and are not being worked up to show condition. They should be kept fit and healthy, but not made too active by the addition of tonic or conditioning seed. The diet should consist of canary seed to provide protein, mixed with cod liver oil emulsion, which adds both fat and vitamins A and D. The oil is mixed in by hand, at the rate of one tablespoonful to a 7.5 liter (2 gal)

bucket of seed. Provided that the weather is cool and that no freak high temperatures are experienced, there is no likelihood of the oil becoming rancid. In a separate container a mixture of millets is offered, consisting of 70 percent *pannicum*, 20 percent *white* and 10 percent *Japanese millet*. Both canary seed and millet seed are replenished as they are eaten. In the early days of the molt it is usual to find that the millets are the favorite food, but as the building phase of growing new feathers arrives, the intake of canary seed becomes very high. It appears that when offered a selection of seeds, the budgerigar chooses what is most likely to be of benefit.

In every season of the year, there must be a plentiful supply of *grit* available to supply the essential minerals and to help the bird to grind up its food. (See entry under *GRIT*.)

Millet sprays can be offered occasionally, just as a tidbit. The budgies love to strip them and then spend endless hours playing with the stalks. They are particularly enjoyed by youngsters.

Greens, especially chickweed, fruit or carrots, are needed to

Two examples of homemade feeding trays grounded on a PVC pipe (top) and on plastic buckets (bottom). These reduce litter when placed inside aviaries.

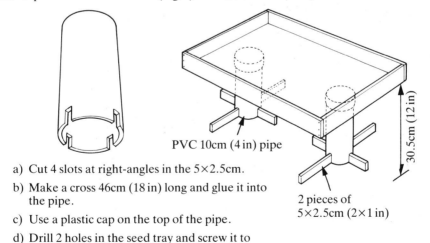

PVC 10cm (4 in) pipe

a) Cut 4 slots at right-angles in the 5×2.5cm.

b) Make a cross 46cm (18 in) long and glue it into the pipe.

c) Use a plastic cap on the top of the pipe.

d) Drill 2 holes in the seed tray and screw it to the top of the pipe to secure.

2 pieces of 5×2.5cm (2×1 in)

30.5cm (12 in)

75cm (30 in)

46cm (18 in)

10cm (4 in)

Place seed trays within tray

23-25cm (9-10 in)

Plastic bucket

Plastic bucket

Cinnamon and opaline cinnamon

Cinnamon grey cock.

Opaline cinnamon light green hen.

A Capern's card showing a cinnamon grey budgerigar.

Opaline cinnamon grey green cock. This bird shows the perfect example of the "powder puff" head so much desired by exhibitors.

supply the necessary vitamins. Make sure that the greens offered have not been frozen or contaminated.

The breeding season places a greater demand upon the birds than any other time of the year. The hen must produce eggs and both cock and hen will feed the chicks. Some budgerigars are so enthusiastic about feeding their young that they can almost starve themselves. Food must always be freely available to them, and extras at this season are highly recommended. The mixed millets and oil-treated canary seed should continue to be given in separate dishes. The recommended amount of oil added to the canary seed should be continued until the second round of eggs has been laid and then gradually reduced over a period of three weeks, after which the oil becomes unnecessary and the canary seed can be fed untreated. Although no research has been carried out on the subject, it has been frequently observed in the authors' birdroom that the pairs who regularly empty the canary-seed pot, eating very little millet, are those who produce a good number of *fertile eggs*, while the pairs which eat mostly mixed millets tend to have a number of *clear eggs* or all clear eggs in their clutches.

There is a definite cycle prior to and during egg laying and hatching. The intake of canary seed remains high until the first chick is ten to fourteen days old and then decreases, with a higher intake of millets. When the chick is four to five weeks old and egg laying begins again, the pair switch back to their preference for canary seed.

Soaked oats are an additional food supply which the birds greatly enjoy and which can be fed three days prior to the time the first egg is due to hatch. The oats should be soaked for 24 to 30 hours and the water changed several times, particularly in hot weather. A bucket which facilitates the soaking of seed is described under *EQUIPMENT*. The soaked oats can be given immediately, but within 48 hours both sprouts and roots will begin to grow and at this stage the birds will devour them with great enthusiasm. Two heaped teaspoonfuls of soaked oats is a reasonable daily ration for a pair and this can be doubled as the chicks hatch. Early morning is the best time to feed oats, so that they can be eaten during the day and none is left to go stale overnight. Once the chicks have been taken away, the oats can be discontinued for four to seven days. The chicks are given soaked oats until they are around sixteen weeks old, but should then be gradually weaned off them by feeding them every other day, then perhaps twice a week. If they are given soaked oats for any longer than this, they are liable to form fat and become overweight. It is then difficult to get rid of this sort of bulk.

Another beneficial extra is

Diagram of a home-made feeding tray. Make a wooden box with ½in (1.25 cm) plywood 15in (38 cm) deep. Fit a piece of lumber 4in (10 cm) from the top all around the sides and across the center as a stiffener. Place a piece of weldmesh inside the box and across the top of the wood. Now place the seed dishes on the wire and the husks will fall through the wire grill to be cleaned up later.

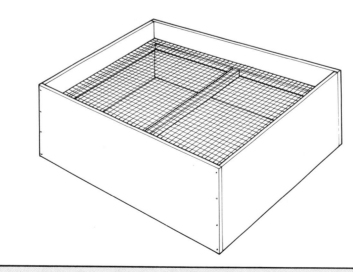

soaked mung beans. They are soaked in the same way as the oats, for 24 to 30 hours, and are then kept in a warm place, such as next to a radiator, for a further twelve hours. They are not as universally popular with the birds as the oats, but once youngsters have had them as part of their diet from birth, they take to them readily. As mung beans add essential vitamins to the diet, it is recommended that a small amount should be offered daily.

One word of caution with all soaked seeds. Always throw away any soaked seed which begins to smell sour or musty. It is far more important to keep the birds healthy and alive than to save a few handfuls of sour oats or mung beans.

A very nutritious softfood, which can be fed each evening in a finger drawer, can be made up in a food processor. Three average-sized raw carrots are processed, four hard-boiled eggs, complete with shells, are added and processed for a few seconds, next three cups of dry wholegrain breadcrumbs and four heaping teaspoons of powdered bee pollen are added and the whole processed for a few more seconds until it becomes a moist and crumbly mixture. This mixture contains almost every nutrient required by the breeding pairs. Bee pollen is nature's most perfect food, containing protein, trace minerals and vitamins including concentrated vitamin E, so vital to high fertility. It is wise to store this in a polyethylene container and keep it in a refrigerator. If only a small number of pairs are kept, then only half the above quantity should be made at one time.

Cuttlefish must always be available, together with a supply of grit.

During the *growing season* the youngsters need to be weaned from all the additives they have had in the breeding cages. Food needs to be more basic, but it must be freely available as it is important for the young birds to maintain their body weight as they grow. They should be given as much canary seed and mixed millet as they can eat, plus occasional millet sprays as a treat. About three times a week, dry oats should be given and will be much enjoyed. Softfood is not advisable at this time, but fresh greens and ripe fruit supply vitamins and are greatly welcomed. The grit dish should be watched and as soon as it becomes fine, it should be thrown away and replaced with a new supply.

During the *show season* the show team are usually kept in stock cages which limits the amount of flying they do. This could lead to their becoming overweight, which spoils the outline of a show bird and frequently becomes permanent. To avoid this, the amount of mixed millets, which contain a high proportion of carbohydrates, should be restricted. Unlimited supplies of canary seed must be available. While greens, fruit and carrot can be offered, exhibitors must be careful not to give these just before a show because they can badly stain the feathers and these stains are sometimes almost impossible to remove. As at any other season of the year, grit must be always provided.

FERTILITY
Fertility is a growing problem among budgerigar breeders. The belief is that the desire for ever bigger and longer birds has led to a smaller number of eggs being fertilized. Another theory is that almost every top-class show bird is related. Over the years, best has been bred to best and those youngsters which have not quite made the grade sold to the breeders a little further down the ladder until, eventually, almost every breeder is inadvertently in-breeding. Whether this belief is true or not has not been proved, but the introduction, from Australia, of the new *spangle mutation* has undoubtedly introduced a new, hybrid vigor into the stock.

FINGER TRAINING
Breeders whose main object is to supply the pet market can, undoubtedly, obtain higher prices

The ino varieties

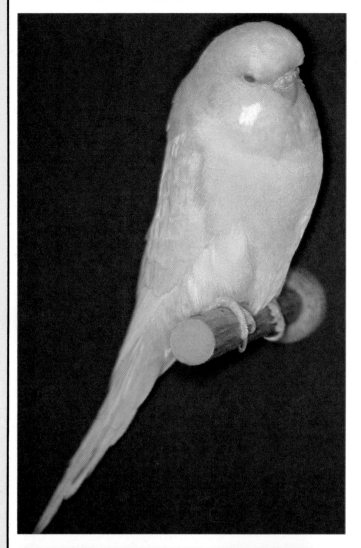

Lutino hen with a good deep golden color.

Two Capern's cards showing a lutino and a cobalt.

Albino hen.

The Australian contrast

Two Australian clearwings, one yellowwing dark green hen and one yellowwing olive hen. The bird on the right appears to be losing a little of the "Australian" contrast.

Two Australian whitewing cobalt hens with brilliant contrast between the white wings and the deep body color.

Budgerigars will treat a finger as another perch if trained properly.

for budgerigars if they, or some member of their family, will undertake the fairly simple and enjoyable task of finger training the birds. Tameness begins in the nest box, and the more chicks are handled at this stage, the sooner they lose any fear of the human hand. Once they leave the nest box the breeder can encourage them to stand on his or her finger or hand by holding millet sprays, pieces of sweet apple, sprays of chickweed or other treats in the hand. When the youngsters are ready to leave their parents and feed independently, it is a good plan to keep them in a normal pet cage to get them used to the sort of environment in which they will be living permanently. If the habit of feeding treats by hand has been followed, it will be found that as a finger is put into the cage, the baby budgies will automatically jump onto it, looking for special treats.

The owner of a new pet which has not been finger trained has a slightly more difficult task, as the youngster's natural nervousness has to be overcome. The owner should stand close to the cage and talk to the bird as often as possible to gain its confidence. Once it has lost its first nervousness, it will

allow the owner to scratch its head. This is an act which budgies seem to enjoy a great deal. This is probably because they can pick at almost any other part of their bodies themselves, but they have to rely on their companions to scratch and pick the top of their heads. In an aviary, this head picking can be seen, with one bird turning and twisting its head for another to scratch every portion. When the bird has learned that fingers seem to be friendly items, which are beneficial rather than fearsome, open the cage and put in a finger, and later the hand. It is important to cover up the opening with the other hand in case the bird tries to fly away. Once the bird has accepted that hands don't hurt and are no menace, the same procedure of offering treats should be followed. When a baby bird realizes that the hand will do it no harm, it accepts the finger as an extension to its other perches and walks onto it quite fearlessly.

FLECKING

Flecking is a fault in exhibition budgerigars and is penalized by the judges. A bird is considered flecked if there are flecks of *melanin* or *striations* on the cap of the bird, which should be clear. This is also referred to as *ticking* or *frosting*, but whatever the name, the penalty is the same. This particular fault has caused more

controversy over the years than any other. Many fanciers have called for a complete ban to be placed on the exhibition of these birds. At one time, no bird demonstrating flecking was allowed to win a first prize. At the moment, the judges are left to decide the degree of penalty which should be awarded, according to the degree of flecking in evidence. It is an offense to try to bleach the black *melanin* from these feathers, or to pluck them out.

FLIGHTS

Ideally, the birdroom should have inside and outside flights. For the inside flight, a frame should be made of 5 × 5 cm (2 × 2 in) lumber with a suitably sized door for you to gain access to the flight, and it is well worth including a small hinged door for returning birds to the flight without the need to open the main door. This will prevent any birds from flying out into the main birdroom. If a solid panel is fitted along the bottom of the flight, this will prevent the husks blowing all over the birdroom. The wooden frame is painted and then covered with strong wire netting, preferably 2 × 2 cm (¾ × ¾ in).

Windows need to be fitted, leading to the outside flights. It is important to position these so that the maximum flying space is available for the birds. It is also important that they are positioned so that the perches are high above the tops of the windows. This eliminates the fear of drafts and reduces the chance of *night fright* due to lights being switched on in a nearby house or a car headlight flashing across the birdroom.

The outside flight should be as large as possible, to give the birds plenty of flying space. Once the size has been determined, a frame is made of 5 × 5 cm (2 × 2 in) lumber or, in larger sizes, 7.5 × 5 cm (3 × 2 in). Make it as strong as possible, particularly in northern climates where it may have to support the weight of snow in winter. Before fixing or fitting the weldmesh, give the frame a good coating of non-toxic wood preservative. Secure 2 × 2 cm (¾ × ¾ in) weldmesh to the frame, giving it two coats of black asphalt paint to protect the wire against rust. Now secure the frame to the birdroom wall at one end and fasten it securely to the ground at the opposite end. It is advisable to dig a trench, 30 cm (12 in) deep, around the flight, then fix some heavy gauge 2.5 × 1.25 cm (1 × ½ in) wire netting from the bottom of the flight frame to the bottom of the trench and then turning outwards, away from the flight, for at least another 23 cm (9 in). The trench should then be filled with gravel. This will deter any vermin. The floor of the outside flight is covered to a depth of 7.5-10 cm (3-4 in) with 2 cm (¾ in) gravel. Again, this is to deter vermin, but it also makes the floor more hygienic, because droppings will wash through. The dampness of the gravel keeps alive grubs which the birds seem to enjoy. In a long dry spell, the gravel can be hosed down, clearing away any accumulated droppings as the water drains away.

Part of the roof should be covered to allow the birds to shelter from heavy rain or hot sun. As soon as it begins to rain, the birds can be seen congregating on the outside wires, enjoying the sensation of getting wet, but they know exactly how wet they want to be and will fly to a sheltered area

Budgerigars showing differing degrees of flecking.

Yellowface
cinnamon opaline
grey cock.

The yellowface variety

The Australian yellowface mauve hen illustrates the intensity of the yellow color in the Australian birds.

Yellowface grey cock.

Yellowface opaline grey hen – note the lack of yellow pigment in the mask.

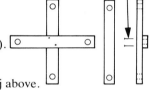

Two methods of making a rotating swing.

a) Cut 2 discs of 1.25cm (½ in) plywood 23cm (9 in) diameter.
b) Drill 4 holes that will take 1.5cm (⅝ in) diameter dowel.
c) Drill 2cm (¾in) center hole to take 1.5cm diameter dowel.
d) Cut 1 piece of 1.5cm (¾ in) dowel 61cm (24 in) long.
e) Cut 4 pieces 1.5cm (⅝ in) dowel 46cm (18 in) long.
f) Fit the 5 pieces of dowel by tapping them into place. Tap thin nails into 2 dowels to lock them into position.
g) Drill a 3mm (⅛in) hole in the center of the 1.5cm (¾in) dowel at each end.
h) Place 2 penny washers on a 4cm (1½in) wood screw. Drive into the ends on the center dowel.
i) Using 3mm (⅛in) galvanized wires hang the swing level from the roof of the outside flight.
j) Loosen the screws slightly until the swing rotates freely.

B. Alternative method
a) Cut 4 pieces of 5×2.5cm (2×1 in) 25cm (10 in) long and drill 2 holes (see b above).
b) Position 2 pieces as a cross and fix with pins.
c) Cut 4 pieces of 1.5cm (⅝ in) dowel (see e above).
d) Fit the 4 pieces of dowel (see f above).
e) Cut off the dowels flush on the outer sides.
f) Fit 2 screws (see h above) and then follow i and j above.

as soon as they have been in the rain long enough. They become bedraggled and unhappy if they cannot escape from heavy rain.

One item which gives the birds endless pleasure, as well as good exercise, is a *rotating swing*. Instructions for making one of these are given at the top of this page.

FLOOR COVERINGS
In a pet cage, the ideal floor covering is the sanded sheets sold for the purpose in all pet shops. Most cages have a sliding tray into which these sand sheets will fit. Some are perforated and are adaptable for any size cage, while others come in various sizes. They are stiff and hard and difficult to break up, which is an advantage when dealing with any of the birds with parrot-type beaks, because tearing things up is part of their recreation. The sheets are very hygienic because they are thrown away after use and all debris and droppings are thrown out with them. An economical floor covering is a sheet of heavy-duty

hard polyethylene cut to size. If this is used, it is as well to have two cut at the same time; then one can be taken out for cleaning and the second one substituted. They should be soaked to loosen the droppings, washed clean and immersed in disinfectant before being reused. Finally, newspaper can be used but the aforesaid tearing habits often result in masses of tiny pieces of newspaper being scattered around the room when the bird flies.

In birdroom and aviary, different types of floor covering are suitable in different areas. Vinyl asbestos tile or linoleum is the best covering for the main birdroom floor, because either is easy to clean with water, they can be very efficiently disinfected, and there are no cracks and crannies for old seed to accumulate in and go moldy, or for seed to fall through and make a feeding ground for vermin.

In the breeding cages, the breeders' personal choice comes into play. The authors recommend the deep litter system and provide a thick layer of sawdust or wood shavings. The wood shavings have the advantage of providing entertainment and relieving boredom, as the birds chew it up into a type of coarse sawdust. The deep litter system provides a soft cushion for the chicks to fall onto when they first come out of the nest box, and is not too unfamiliar from the nest box environment when the chicks come out and huddle together in a corner or behind the seed tray, half hidden in the shavings. Another covering which is used is newspapers, which can be frequently changed, but an endless supply is necessary. Or there are those breeders who prefer no deep litter and leave the floor plain wood with no covering whatsoever.

The inside flights can have a plain concrete floor, which needs scraping and scrubbing to clean it, or a thin layer of sawdust or shavings can be used so that droppings are more easily removed. Some find that the same covering as that of the main birdroom floor is very convenient, as far as cleaning is concerned, but if tile or linoleum is used, it should be stuck down firmly and sealed at the edges, so that water does not get through, causing moldy patches.

The floor of the outside flights can be soil, which is dug over fairly frequently to prevent it from becoming sour through the constant droppings, and to present a fresh layer containing various grubs for the birds: the disadvantage here is that rodents could easily burrow up through the soil. Or the floor can be a deep layer of sand, but in this case the sand, if sea sand, should be well washed before use to clean out all the salt. Unfortunately, sand washes away fairly quickly and needs frequent replenishing. The recommended covering is coarse gravel which can be shoveled over and washed through with disinfectant, then rinsed with clear water to keep them clean and hygienic.

FRENCH MOLT
Much research has taken place into the possible cause of this disease and many theories have been propounded. One group of fanciers support the theory that the cause is some deficiency, or even excess, in the diet; others are convinced that a virus is the cause. Lack of protein, overdosage of vitamins, the inability of the hen to produce crop milk, even the presence of moths in the birdroom have all been blamed for outbreaks of the disease, and innumerable "cures" have been recommended, but there presently is no cure.

French molt usually becomes apparent in the nest box at any time after the feathers have begun to form. In severe cases, the feathers begin to drop when the chick is little over two weeks old: tiny, half-formed feathers will be

French molt is an inexplicable condition, the cause of which is still unknown.

noticed in the nest box and the poor chick continues to drop its feathers as soon as they grow, making it a pathetic, almost naked creature when it is ready to leave the nest box. Birds affected to this extent seldom recover and it is kinder to put them to sleep humanely. In milder cases, the chick begins to lose its feathers just before or just after it leaves the box. The flights and tail feathers are those most likely to be affected. These youngsters are unable to fly until they have regrown the feathers, and should be kept in a stock cage, with water

Clearwings

Whitewing skyblue budgerigar.

British whitewing cobalt cock which demonstrates how some of the color contrast has been lost in the quest for size.

British yellow-wing dark green hen.

British whitewing skyblue cock.

British yellowface skyblue cock.

Left: A yellowface skyblue budgerigar on a Capern's card.

Far left: Whitewing cobalt budgerigar.

and seed available somewhere low enough for them to reach it, until they are able to fly with ease.

In yet another form of the disease, all the feathers grow normally, the youngsters leave the nest box fully fledged, and then, without warning, some, or all, of the flight and tail feathers suddenly drop off. As with the chicks described above, these birds, even if they have been allowed into the flights, should be returned to a stock cage to regrow their full complement of feathers.

FRONTAL RISE

This is a term used to describe the way in which a budgerigar is able to display the rise of its feathers from the top of the cere to the center of its head. A tightly tucked-in beak with an exaggerated circle of feathers rising to the top of the head is greatly admired in show circles.

A superb cock budgerigar lifting its head feathers to display its frontal rise.

G

GENERAL COUNCIL

The general council of the Budgerigar Society (UK) is the governing body of the budgerigar fancy in Britain. The members formulate the rules under which shows are run, the general rules of the society and the standards for the many varieties of birds which are exhibited. There are 40 members; two are sent as delegates from each area society and the remaining twenty are chosen by ballot each year. All paid-up members are eligible to vote and are provided with a ballot form annually. The elected members serve a term of two years before re-election; therefore ten are elected in each year's ballot. Meetings of the general council are held twice yearly unless emergency meetings are required. The May meetings move from one area society to another each year, which means there will be ten different venues. This allows as many members as possible the opportunity of attending an annual general meeting. The meetings in October alternate between the north and south of the country. Sub-committees are chosen to administer finance, judges and color standards, the world championship show and any other activity in which a subcommittee is considered appropriate.

GENES

Genes are units of inheritance. They affect every aspect of every person or animal. In budgerigars the genes about which we know most are those which affect color. We know that if a bird is green, one of the parents was carrying a "green gene." What is not generally realized, and has not been studied in depth, as far as is known, is that everything – length of feather, size, size of spots, position of beak or eye – is carried in the genes of the bird.

GENETICS

Genetics is the science of inheritance. It is a complex subject which deserves a book of its own and several excellent volumes on the subject are available. In budgerigars, the science of genetics is used, in the main, to forecast the expectations of colors or varieties. A large number of facts are accepted by even the newest beginner, but not so many understand the method by which the laws of color inheritance work. The simplest method of learning about this subject is to make a chart using letters to indicate the colors. It is rare to find a pure bird which has not been mated with another color and is, therefore, not carrying the other color in a split form. However, let us imagine that we have a pure unsplit green bird to mate to a pure unsplit blue. Let XX stand for a cock and XY for a hen, G for green and B for blue. A chart could be prepared as follows:

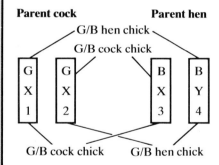

Each of the parents is carrying two potentials for color. If we take potential number 1 from the cock, with potential number 3 from the hen, we produce a green youngster which is split for blue. As green is dominant to blue, the bird will be visibly green, but carrying a hidden (or split) potential for blue. Take potential number 2 from the cock, with number 4 from the hen, and you arrive at the same result, as would 1 and 4, or 2 and 3. It is impossible to breed from this pair anything but green birds carrying a blue split.

Now, if we mate together two of the split birds we have produced, the chart would read:

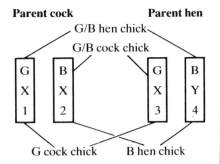

We take potential number 1 from the cock and number 3 from the hen. They are both green, they are both Xs, and so we have produced a green cock. If we take 1 from the cock with 4 from the hen, we have one G and one B, one X and one Y, which means we have bred a green/blue (visual green) hen. Take number 2 from the cock with number 3 from the hen and we have two Xs again, which means another cock, and this time a B and a G. Since green is dominant over blue, we would again have a visually green bird with a hidden blue potential. Finally, however, potential number 2 from the cock could tie up with number 4 from the hen, both Bs, and this would give us a pure blue hen.

Using this very simple method, giving each color or variety a different initial, all the color expectations can be worked out.

Unfortunately, other factors can complicate matters. The opaline factor, cinnamon, lutino, albino, lacewing and slate factors are all *sex-linked*, that is, the factor cannot be carried by the Y potential of the hen. The *opaline factor*, designated O, can be carried by either of the two Xs of the cock. A chart to prove this theory, based on two green/blue birds, the cock being a split opaline and the hen an opaline, would look like this:

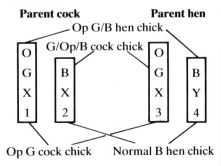

If we take 1 from the cock carrying the O factor, with 3 from the hen, we have OGX and OGX, or in other words, an opaline green cock.

Potential number 2 from the cock, with number 3 from the hen, gives BX and OGX, a split opaline cock, but this time it is green/blue. Potential number 1 from the cock carrying the opaline potential, with 4 from the hen, would result in OGX and BY. The resulting chick would be a hen, it would be visibly green, but split for blue, *and it would be an opaline*. While the cock needs two opaline factors for the opaline to be visible, a hen is a visible opaline if it has any opaline factor. If number 2 from the cock joined with number 4 from the hen, a non-opaline hen would be the result. The O factor, which is floating, could also combine with potential number 2.

C for cinnamon could be substituted for the O for opaline and the same result would be achieved. In the same way, expectations for lutino, albino, slate and lacewing can also be worked out.

For those who find the whole subject too perplexing, charts giving every possible mating have been worked out by Dr. D. H. Duncker and are incorporated in the book *Budgerigar Mating and Colour Expectations*, published by the Budgerigar Society.

A table for cinnamons, which would apply to all sex-linked varieties is given below.

GREENS

This is rather a loose term as various vegetables can be included under this description. Care must be taken when feeding any form of greens. The food must be fresh, must be uncontaminated by animals or garden sprays and should be given regularly. It should not be given in excess and any left over at the end of a day must be removed.

Chickweed is the greens most enjoyed by budgerigars particularly when it is in bud, as the buds are full of a nutritious milky sap. In Australia, and for that matter anywhere that the trees can be persuaded to grow, eucalyptus leaves are the greatest treat. Cabbage, spinach, lettuce, parsley, dandelion leaves, sweet apple, carrots and beetroot are all taken with enjoyment. While budgerigars do not normally overeat, if large amounts are available, they will eat more greens than is good for them, resulting in diarrhea; therefore the breeder must ration the supply. A small handful in the breeding cages is ample. In flights, bunches can be hung up or put on shelves, but the

SEX-LINKED VARIETIES

MATINGS		EXPECTATIONS	
Cock	**Hen**	**Cocks**	**Hens**
1 Cinnamon × Non-Cinnamon		Split Cinnamon	Cinnamon
2 Cinnamon × Cinnamon		Cinnamon	Cinnamon
3 Split Cinnamon × Non-Cinnamon		Split Cinnamon and Non-Cinnamon	Cinnamon and Non-Cinnamon
4 Split Cinnamon × Cinnamon		Cinnamon and Split-Cinnamon	Cinnamon and Non-Cinnamon
5 Non-Cinnamon × Cinnamon		Split Cinnamon	Non-Cinnamon

Hens cannot be split for any sex-linked variety.

amounts should be limited.

It is better to give root vegetables in dishes to avoid them being dragged around the floor and possibly fouled with droppings. Most root vegetables are better fed grated. Eating greens can result in staining of the facial feathers and mask and so they should not be given to birds just before a show. While all the greens left over must be removed in the evening so that they cannot putrify overnight and be consumed by the birds in that state in the morning, the stems of cabbage or spinach can be left because they do not rot so quickly and the birds love to play with them. An excellent way to feed greens is to contact a firm supplying powdered grass and to add a heaping teaspoon of this to the oil-treated canary seed. This can supply all the necessary vitamins to breeding pairs.

The vital rules again are: *not frozen, not contaminated, not stale and not a lot!* (See *CHICKWEED* and *GROUNDSEL*.)

GREY FACTOR

The grey factor is often misunderstood. Because a bird carrying two grey factors will always produce all grey progeny, it has been thought that grey is a new color, but it is not. Every visual grey bird is a blue series bird which has been modified by one or two grey factors. If the bird is carrying the grey in a single factor, and is mated to a blue bird, the youngsters may be grey or blue, but if the grey bird is carrying two grey factors, then all the offspring will be visually grey but will be carrying only one grey factor. Equally, if the grey bird is mated with a green, then the grey factor will modify the green, turning it into grey green. The grey factor can be introduced into all the varieties and colors and will modify them all in the same manner: all the birds of the blue series will lose their original color and appear grey, while the green series will change their original shade to a more muted shade with grey.

GRIT

Grit is essential to the budgerigar for the digestion of its food. One portion of the gizzard consists of two hardened pads especially designed for grinding together the seed and grit. Grit must therefore always be available to the birds, who will know themselves how much they need and take it accordingly. Unfortunately, the birds are both playful and naturally destructive and will reduce the grit into a fine dust within a short time, so that it is necessary to inspect the grit dishes regularly, throw away the fine dust and replenish with a coarser grit. A good mixture can be made from oyster shell, limestone, mineral grit, large pigeon grit and large grains of sea sand from a clean beach which have been washed clean of salt.

GROUNDSEL

This is a weed which is enjoyed by most budgies, but, as with all other

A sprig of groundsel.

kinds of greens, care must be taken to see that it has not been contaminated. If there is any likelihood that cats or other pets could have sprayed it with urine or, if growing wild in hedgerows, that it could have been sprayed with weed-killer or car exhaust fumes, then it should not be used. It is not safe in this state, however much it is washed before use. (See also *GREENS*.)

H

HAND REARING
Sometimes, if both parents have died and there are no other pairs breeding with which you can foster the chick or chicks, or if for some reason the parents reject one particular youngster, it becomes necessary to try to rear the chick by hand. This is a task which requires a great deal of patience and dedication, but it can be done. A hand-reared chick, rather than a discarded dead youngster, from a breeding pair from whom the breeder expected his or her best results, is a great source of satisfaction. The older the baby is when hand-rearing commences, the more chance there is of success.

The baby bird is normally kept warm by the hen, at first tucked right underneath her where the temperature is around 32° C (90° F), and later close to her in a temperature of about 30° C (86° F). Some sort of substitute has to be found for this environment and it is unlikely that the average fancier has anything purpose-made available. A plastic cake tin with the lid left slightly open, and lined with crumpled tissues, is a possibility. This must be kept somewhere where the temperature can be controlled at that at which the chick appears comfortable. If it is too hot it will move about, lifting its wings, trying to get cool. If it is too cold, it will soon die. A thermometer, which can be checked constantly, is a necessity. If a hospital cage is available, the chick can be housed in a plastic basin which has first been warmed and then lined with tissues, and a tissue can be put on top of the chick. A bowl of water should be placed near the basin to prevent the air becoming too dry.

The following dry mixture should be reduced to a fine powder in a blender, then mixed with hot water to a thin cream and a tiny drop of a multivitamin added. The ingredients can be obtained in a health food store.

3 tablespoons high protein baby cereal
1 tablespoon wheat germ
1 tablespoon millet meal
1 tablespoon sunflower meal

This is given with a pipette and can be squirted directly down the gullet, which saves a lot of time, although it can be dangerous if any of the food should get into the windpipe. It is far better to let the baby suck it from the pipette itself, held to the beak, but a lot of patience is needed. It helps if the chick is held with a tissue wrapped around it to prevent any of the feed spilling onto the feathers, as it is sticky and sets fairly hard. The number of feeds needed per day depends upon the age of the chick. When very tiny, it needs to be fed almost every two hours during the day, and several times during the night, but when it is about three weeks old, once every four hours, with a late night and early morning feed, is plenty. After a few days, most youngsters can be persuaded to take the food from a spoon with the sides bent up to form a kind of scoop, which speeds up the feeding time required considerably.

Any food not used at one feed should be kept in the refrigerator and reheated when required. A suitable receptable is the indentation in an egg poacher, and this cup, or eggcup, in which it is stored can be placed in a saucepan of boiling water until it reaches the right temperature. The food should be fairly warm but not so hot that it will burn the throat of the baby. The best method of testing is a few drops on one's own tongue. It is quite palatable.

HEAD QUALITY
The shape of the head plays an important part in deciding whether a bird will make a good show specimen. The spots may be large, the mask deep, the color superlative, but unless the head is wide when viewed face on, has a frontal rise which continues in a graceful sweep over the top of the

A bird with all the desirable head qualities.

head and does not fall away at the back, it is unlikely to win against reasonable competition.

HEATING
From many observations and experiments, it appears that artificial heating is not absolutely essential, as budgerigars seem to be able to breed successfully in revolutionary new theory linking ancient very low temperatures. Some form of heating is desirable in colder areas, however, for two reasons. Occasionally, temperatures plummet to well below zero and this can hardly be comfortable for very young babies; also, if the temperature is kept at around 10° C (50° F), the birdroom is certainly far more comfortable for the fancier. Birds in inside flights with access to outside flights do not require any heating, but care must be taken to check that the water supply has not frozen.

Oil stoves and gas heaters should never be used for heating aviaries or birdhouses. Horror stories of birdrooms where the wicks of oil heaters have blown out, filling the room with filthy smoke which has slowly and painfully choked the lungs of the poor birds, until they have been found dead or dying in the morning, used to be heard in the past. Fortunately, almost every fancier has learned that the only

safe methods of heating a birdroom are electric tubular heaters, electric oil-filled radiators, or some form of central heating radiators as an extension from the central heating of the house. Whichever of these is used, it should be controlled by a thermostat. Unless the birdroom has been efficiently insulated, heating can be an expensive item.

HOBBY see *FANCY*.

HOSPITAL CAGE
A commercially bought hospital cage is a small all-metal cage with a built-in heater and thermostat. Being of metal, it is easy to clean fastidiously and to disinfect. Its one disadvantage is that it is an alien environment for the sick bird and therefore likely to cause *stress*. A bird which is very ill has little interest in its surroundings, but if the bird is just "off-color," it may be more beneficial to use a show cage with which it is familiar and to put this in a warm place. An ordinary thermometer can be used to try to ensure that the temperature is kept at around 29° C (85° F). Because heat tends to make a budgie thirsty, as does fever, a supply of water must always be available and if this is treated with any medicine, it is necessary to anticipate that the bird will drink more than usual and to adjust the dose accordingly. A shallow container of water should

A hospital cage should be warm, but must never be too hot.

be kept near the cage to counteract the air-drying effect of the heat of the hospital cage, or nearby fire or radiator. One word of warning: before leaving a cage in front of direct heat, first check the intensity of the heat by holding the back of your hand in front of the cage, between the cage and the heat source, for about five minutes. If it is uncomfortable for your hand, it will be uncomfortable for the bird, and the cage should be moved back.

HUMIDITY

A degree of humidity is needed to keep the eggs from drying so much that the membranes just inside the shell toughen, making it impossible for the chick to break out of the shell, resulting in a lot of chicks *dead in shell*. In most areas the temperature range is such, and the rainfall high enough, to make any additional form of humidity not an absolute necessity. However, in particularly dry seasons, or if the breeder decides to pair up the birds in the summer for some reason, and in many other countries, it is necessary to install a *humidifier* and *humidistat* to control the humidity of the air.

The vital humidity is that underneath the hen, but many believe that this is affected by the general humidity of the surrounding atmosphere.

HUSBANDRY

From the very first day of keeping birds, a routine should be established. The birds become used to it, it means that essential tasks are never overlooked and very often disasters can be avoided. If your hours of work permit, it is wise to visit the birdroom or aviary twice each day, once in the morning and again in early evening. First check over the outside of the flights, looking for any structural damage caused by cats, dogs or other visitors. Check that the wire netting is intact and there is nowhere that a bird could escape. Next, look along the perches at the birds to ensure that none are sitting hunched up, usually with head tucked around

and both feet down. If there are, make a note of which ones they are and remember to take action as soon as you are inside the birdhouse. Next, look around the floor to make certain there are no sick or even dead birds lying anywhere.

Now go into the birdroom and carry out the same checks in the inside flights. If you discover any birds which look sick, catch them and put each in a clean show cage or hospital cage. Cover the floor of the cage with dry seed and twist a millet spray around the bars. Fill a drinking fountain with water and fix this so that it can be reached even if the bird does not sit on the perch. Place the cage near a radiator or any other place where it will remain quite warm, but not uncomfortably so – and then wash your hands thoroughly. (Hands should always be washed, preferably with disinfectant in the water, after handling a sick or dead bird.)

The bird should be observed carefully over the next few hours. If it appears to be recovering, as they often do when kept in a warm place, leave it for two days and then move it further and further from the heat, until it is once again used to the sort of temperature at which you keep your birdroom, before releasing it back into the birdroom. If it shows no sign of recovery and symptoms appear to indicate a serious illness, the advice of a veterinary surgeon should be sought.

Once the health of the birds has been checked and any invalids have been ministered to, the seed dishes should be checked and refilled where necessary, then any soaked seeds or additives distributed. It is sensible to have feeding dishes which are large enough to avoid having to replenish them daily, both because the task is time-consuming and also in case of some emergency which might prevent you from visiting the birdroom on a particular day. Always start and finish your rounds at the same spot.

Once each week the flights should be cleaned of dust and all droppings removed. During the breeding season, the copious droppings of the hens should also be removed from the breeding cages.

Once every three months, one flight at a time should be emptied of birds and cleaned thoroughly with water to which a chlorous type of disinfectant has been added. Walls, perches and floor should be washed.

To prevent mite and any build up of moths or other insects, twice a year, preferably in late spring and early autumn, the inside flights, after removal of the birds, should be sprayed with one of the special sprays sold for this purpose. The smell of this is dreadful, but it does prevent any sign of mite. No birds should be returned to the flight until it is completely dry.

Once breeding has been completed and the birds transferred to the flights, the breeding cages should be brushed out, scrubbed, disinfected and painted with paint which has been mixed with one of the anti-mite products.

I

IDEAL BUDGERIGAR
Most budgerigar societies throughout the world describe or illustrate a standard of excellence for what they consider to be the ideal budgerigar. The differences in the written descriptions are usually minor, while the pictorial representation can differ according to the interpretation of the artist. The American Budgerigar Society uses the standard set by the UK Budgerigar Society which reads as follows:

CONDITION is essential. If a bird is not in condition it should *never* be considered for any award.

TYPE – Gracefully tapered from nape of neck to tip of tail, with an approximately straight back line and a rather deep, nicely curved chest.

LENGTH – The ideal length is eight-and-a-half inches [22 cm] from the crown of the head to the tip of the tail.

WINGS – Carried just above the cushion of the tail and not crossed. The ideal length of the wing is three-and-three-quarter inches [9.5 cm] from the butt to the tip of the longest primary flight which must contain seven visual primary flight feathers fully grown.

HEAD – Large, round, wide and symmetrical when viewed from any angle; curvature of skull commencing at cere, to lift outward and upward, continuing over the top and to the base of head in one graceful sweep.

BEAK – Set well into the face.

EYE – To be bold and bright and positioned well away from the front, top and back skull.

NECK – To be short and wide when viewed from either side or front.

TAIL – To be straight and tight with two long tail feathers.

POSITION – Steady, on perch, at an angle of 30 degrees from the vertical, looking fearless and natural.

These wooden models by R. Harris depict his interpretation of the ideal shape of a cock and hen. The male has a noticeably deeper chest.

MASK AND SPOTS – Mask to be clear, deep and wide, and where demanded by the Standards should be ornamented by six evenly spaced large round throat spots, the outer two being partially covered at the base of cheek patches, the size of spots to be in proportion to the rest of the make-up of the bird.

LEGS AND FEET – Legs should be straight and strong, with two front and two rear toes and claws firmly gripping perch.

MARKINGS – Wavy markings on cheek, head, neck, back and wings to stand out clearly.

COLOR – Clear and level and of an even shade.

INBREEDING

Inbreeding should never be attempted by beginners, because while it may stabilize desirable features carried by the parents, it can also double up on any faults they may be carrying, some of which may be hidden. The mating of mother to son, father to daughter, brother to sister, or first cousin to first cousin is what is understood as inbreeding. Mating of more distantly related birds comes under the heading of *linebreeding*. A very careful check should be made by those practicing inbreeding that the stock which they use is selected for fertility. If inbreeding is used on stock already showing poor fertility, this feature will be exaggerated as each generation is inbred, until eventually no further progeny will be produced because the birds will have become sterile.

The aim of inbreeding is to increase and then stabilize particular desirable features in a fancier's stock. He or she may, for example, have a bird with very large, perfectly round and even spots which he or she wishes to stabilize into his or her stud – and this is possible. The fancier should, however, be conversant with the history of the large-spotted bird and should not attempt to commence inbreeding with it unless detailed records have been kept. If some hereditary defect were to be carried by this bird and also by its partner, then, as well as large spots, the breeder might be introducing flecked heads or poor markings or some other fault. Provided that the breeder is experienced and has kept meticulous records, he or she may achieve surprising improvements in show quality by inbreeding. This has been demonstrated particularly in South Africa, where there are few breeders and they were unable to import outcrosses to improve their stock.

The beginner to inbreeding should choose very carefully the birds with which he or she intends to establish a family. Having chosen a pair, he or she should look back through the records to find out if any faults have been recorded – in appearance, in breeding habits – or if any weaknesses have appeared regularly for several years. Any bird without an excellent pedigree should be discarded. If an *outcross* is being sought, it should be explained to the seller that the purpose is to start inbreeding and he or she should be asked to search his or her records to make sure that the bird being bought has a good pedigree. After the first breeding season, the youngsters should be examined carefully. Any displaying any of the major faults should be discarded from the future breeding team.

Once the birds have molted and are in their full adult plumage, the wisest plan is to cage each family, parents and offspring, to judge what progress, if any, has been made. If the youngsters are an improvement on their parents and are carrying no major faults, then it is safe to continue with that family as part of your inbreeding team. If, on the other hand, the progeny are of poorer quality than their parents, or have crossed wings, drooping tails, heavy flecking, or any bad show point, they should be ruthlessly discarded.

INCUBATION

The normal period of incubation for a budgerigar egg is eighteen days. Eggs are laid on alternate days and, subsequently, also hatch every other day. Usually the hen starts to incubate the egg as soon as it has been laid, but there are always exceptions to the rule and some hens will lay two or three eggs before starting to incubate, which can interfere with the sequence of hatching.

There is very little likelihood of difficulty during the incubation period. Provided that the hen is fit, she will sit quite contentedly in the nest box, coming out only to feed or defecate. The cock, as a general rule, sits outside in the breeding cage, feeds the hen and, when she emerges from the nest box is attentive and affectionate. Sometimes a cock will stay in the box with the hen, quite quietly and seemingly quite welcome. On very rare occasions, a cock will become troublesome, disturbing the hen so constantly that she is unable to incubate the eggs and becomes quarrelsome. If this is observed, it is better to remove the cock for most of each day and, if the trouble continues even after the chicks begin to hatch, when he should be kept busy feeding the hen, he can be removed altogether and the hen allowed to bring up the chicks on her own. In this case, it is wise to foster some of the chicks when they are old enough to band, leaving the hen with only two chicks to rear.

Hens can hatch and have hatched clutches of up to nine eggs, although four or five are more usual. As the temperature just around the hen is considerably lower than the temperature just underneath her, where she actually incubates, it is not surprising that eggs which are on the perimeter of her so-called "incubation pad" fail to hatch.

INFERTILITY

The causes of infertility are many, and very often a pair who have not produced are wrongly labelled infertile. As more research is carried out into the production of eggs and the reasons for eggs being *addled* or *dead in shell*, and even, recently, into *artificial insemination*, many new facts have emerged. It has been found that the cocks have a cycle during part of which they produce either no sperm or immature sperm. At this time the testes are tiny, in comparison to what is needed to produce the semen alive with sperm, which is needed to ensure the fertilization of the egg. If the cock is put down to breed during the "resting" period, he is unlikely to fertilize the hen's eggs and may, mistakenly, be thought to be infertile. Two things help to bring him back into breeding condition; extra light and the call of the hen. Extra artificial lighting can help with both, since the hen will call more often during the hours of light.

One of the other reasons for apparent infertility is that the

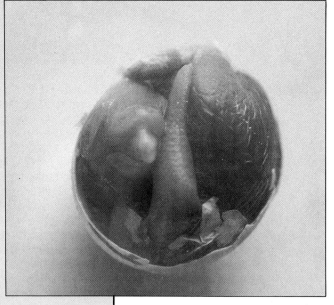

An unborn chick that is dead in its shell.

perches in the breeding cage may be too smooth. If round doweling is used for perches, sometimes the hen is unable to grip the perch and the cock literally falls off before copulation can occur. The answer to this problem is to fit square perches.

Coarse feathering around the hen's vent area can sometimes prevent efficient copulation, no matter how fertile the pair. One possible answer to this is to pluck the feathers away from the vent area – very, very carefully – or to trim them with scissors.

There are other reasons for *clear*, or apparently clear, eggs. Some infection may be present in the nest box which kills off the embryo before it can start to develop; or the hen may not be incubating properly because she is being disturbed by the cock, by mice in the birdroom, or by flashing lights or unusual night

noises. All possible causes should be examined before a bird is dubbed infertile.

INO FACTOR
The ino factor has the effect of masking all the genes of the green series birds, to produce the lutino, and all the genes of the blue series birds, except one, to produce the albino. The one gene in the blue series which the ino factor seems incapable of masking is the yellow face. When these two genes are present in one bird, a yellowface albino is the result. Although the ino gene appears to be dominant to all colors, it does not affect varieties. Tufted or crested lutinos and albinos are quite commonplace.

INSULATION
The heat loss from a birdroom or aviary which is not insulated is very considerable. A thick layer of insulation between the outer and inner walls and the roof space is a good long-term investment. Care must be taken not to use an insulating material which could become a warren of nests for rodents this is prevented by using a material a material which would be very uncomfortable, such as rock wool or fiberglass.

INTERMEDIATE
An intermediate is an exhibitor who has passed through the novice section. To advance from the novice to intermediate division, the exhibitor must have shown birds at three different shows with at least five exhibitors in the novice division. He or she must have won a first, second or third best novice award, one of which must have been a first best novice. Only one win per competition can be counted and this must be in open competition. Parlor shows, baby shows, invitational shows, or any shows where the entry is restricted, cannot be counted. All wins must have been with birds bred and banded by the exhibitor. Once an exhibitor has moved up from novice to intermediate, he or she cannot drop back into the lower division.

J

JUDGES' CLINICS

At every regional show, the ABS judge or judges engaged are required to organize a judges' clinic, and all judges exhibiting at, or attending the show are expected to attend. The objective of these clinics is to develop a uniform perception of exhibition budgerigars and more closely understand the ABS standards of perfection. The presiding judge is then required to make a full report of the clinic to the ABS judges' panel committee.

JUDGES' PANELS

In the US the would-be judge has to apply to the ABS to become a judge trainee, having first obtained sponsorship from an ABS affiliated club. The applicant must have bred and raised budgerigars for a minimum period of five years and have exhibited his or her entries in the champion section at ABS patronage shows for a minimum period of three years, gaining at least one top award with different birds at these shows.

The apprenticeship begins by a trainee accompanying a judge throughout a show, and finishes by taking a practical test in which he or she is asked to judge three different classes or sections with five different groups of birds, while the judge is out of the room, recording the results which are kept confidential. The official judge then judges the same classes and records his or her results. The two papers are sent to an evaluating panel who notify the applicant of his success or failure. The trainee judge is allowed two years in which to qualify. If anyone fails to qualify within the allotted period, he or she must start again.

In the UK, there are two levels of judges; the subsidiary panel, whose members are allowed, individually, to judge shows at a lower patronage level, and the main panel. To achieve subsidiary panel status, a person must have been a member of the Budgerigar Society for not less than ten years and must be currently exhibiting as a champion. To reach the standard needed for the main panel, a person must have judged at least nine classes over three years, under the supervision of main panel judges, and then pass both practical and written examinations. Once elevated to the main panel, the judge must continue to breed and exhibit birds annually, and must remain a paid-up member of the Budgerigar Society.

JUDGING RULES

Each country differs slightly in its judging rules, but all endeavor to ensure absolute fairness for the exhibitors. Cages are recognized only by cage numbers or tags which give no indication of the owner of the bird and no judge is allowed to discover the owners until after all judging has been completed. In the UK judges are not allowed to stay overnight with an exhibitor before a show, and it would be unethical for a judge to visit an exhibitor's birdroom where he or she might see the exhibits. A bird cannot be exhibited if it was bought from the judge who will be adjudicating at the show, and no judge is allowed to show budgerigars at a show at which he or she is adjudicating, even if scheduled to judge a different color or section. The only exception to this rule is that a subsidiary panel judge may exhibit at a show at which he is training.

JUNIORS

Exhibitors are allowed to show in the junior division until they attain their sixteenth birthdays. All birds shown in this division must be bred and banded by the exhibitor, with bands obtained from the ABS. A junior may not enter birds in the novice division at any show which has a junior division, and then drop back. The junior members are not allowed to vote at meetings or in ballots for officers or district directors.

L

LACEWINGS

As the name implies, the markings on a lacewing are lighter than those of the normal varieties. They are red-eyed, sex-linked birds with a clear body color of yellow or white and light cinnamon markings on head, neck, mask and wings. Although of attractive appearance, these birds have not become popular on the show bench because they tend to be much smaller than their normal counterparts.

LAYING, SIGNS OF

Once the birds have been paired up and a nest box provided, if all is well, the hen will begin to investigate the nest box. Her visits will become more frequent and the periods spent inside will become longer. Sometimes the fancier sees mating taking place, but not always, and this is not important. Remember, no one can be watching for 24 hours a day. Two of the telltale signs that the hen will soon lay are that she begins to tap on the nest box walls and she attempts to chew the nest-box hole. At the lower part of the hen's body, behind the legs, it will become noticeable (usually on the sixth or seventh day after pairing) that the area is slightly enlarged and, at the same time, the droppings will change from the normal, small black-and-white pieces to much heavier, softer deposits, roughly six times larger than during the rest of the year. These heavy droppings will continue throughout the laying and incubation period, allowing the hen to remain in the nest box for long periods without the need to come out to defecate.

LEGS

The legs of a young budgerigar are usually a light, fleshy color. With the normal varieties they darken as they become older, until, at about one year old, they are greyish with a much rougher surface. The legs of a young budgerigar are fragile and easily damaged. While in the nest box they may become fouled by excreta which quickly hardens. This should not be picked off, because it is so easy to break or hurt a leg. It can, however, be soaked off quite easily using a piece of soft cloth and warm water.

Problems with the legs can sometimes arise as the birds get older. A piece of sawdust, grit, scale or other foreign body can get caught inside the closed band. This can make a tiny abrasion which becomes infected, resulting in a swollen leg. If this goes undetected, the bird could be lost or, at the least, suffer a great deal of pain and discomfort. Observing the birds for any signs of illness or discomfort is always very important.

If a bird with a swollen leg is discovered, iodine ointment should be applied twice daily and a hot wet cloth held around the leg as a poultice for about five minutes. If, after two days, the swelling has not reduced, the band should be cut off. A pair of very short nail clippers is a very useful tool for this task. Anyone without experience should not attempt to cut off a band because it is possible to break the leg or cause excess bleeding. Help should be sought from an experienced breeder or from a veterinary surgeon. When cutting off a band, the band should be held absolutely steady in a pair of narrow pliers. If it should twist, it could break the leg or pierce the swollen flesh. It is always useful to have a second person to hold the bird for this operation. It is advisable to make two cuts and the two portions will then come away quite easily.

If a sitting hen should develop a swollen leg, the band should be cut off as soon as this is noticed since it is not feasible to keep her under supervision and observe the progress she is making

Once bands are removed, it is no longer possible to win some awards, but the health and comfort of the birds must come first.

LICE
Known as *feather lice*, these parasites burrow to the base of the feathers and can cause tremendous irritation. A bird infected with these lice will continually pick at its feathers, to such an extent that bare patches will appear. It is very difficult to trace the lice, as they live beneath the feathers, close to the skin. If the condition is suspected, the bird should be washed daily in warm soapy water to which a mild disinfectant has been added, taking care not to allow this to get into the eyes. Eight or nine days are usually sufficient to clear the lice. The patient's partner should also be observed for signs of feather picking. If necessary, it too should be treated. The nest box should be sprayed with a strong *anti-mite solution* before the birds are put in again. If the affected bird has come from the main flights, then all the others should be watched for signs of lice and the flight thoroughly cleaned, disinfected and sprayed with an anti-mite solution.

LIGHTiNG
Lighting is almost a necessity, to enable the breeder to tend to the needs of his or her stock during the winter months before he or she goes to work and after he or she returns. It is also an aid to giving more hours of light to the birds, which helps to bring them into breeding condition. It is advisable to have a 1.5 m (5 ft) fluorescent fitting for every 2.5 m (8 ft) in length of the birdroom. A *night light* is not a luxury; it can help settle the birds down during a storm or any other disturbance, and allows the breeding hen sufficient light to find food during the night when she is feeding young chicks. The most useful types of night lights are those which connect to the mains, but have a built-in transformer which reduces the voltage to 12v or 6v. This also reduces the amount of heat, which is a safety factor. Unless you are a competent electrician you should not attempt to install this wiring. Instead, engage a licensed electrician.

LINE BREEDING
Descriptions of line breeding often differ very little from *in-breeding*, but the generally accepted view is that line breeding means using birds not quite so closely related. Mother to son, father to daughter or sister to brother are accepted as inbreeding, while cousin to aunt or uncle, half sister to half brother, etc., are believed to be line breeding. The same rules apply to both. The breeder must be experienced before attempting this type of breeding, and must have available to him or her comprehensive records going back for several generations, giving information on any fault which may have been carried by the family. Once two or three lines, or families, have been established, the best progeny of each are mated together to produce a better quality of show stock than the original pairings. As the relationships used in line breeding are not close, the procedure can be carried on for a number of generations before the lines become too closely interrelated and new families need to be established.

LIST OF MEMBERS
For beginners coming into the budgerigar fancy, or for any member who is traveling, a list of other members is of immense interest. The American Budgerigar Society, and a number of other overseas budgerigar clubs, have lists of members available for members and visitors to their countries. In the UK the Budgerigar Society publishes a handbook which gives the names and addresses of all members. As many keen overseas fanciers are members of the UK Budgerigar Society, even those traveling overseas are able to contact fellow fanciers on their journeys, and often do so.

LOSS OF FEATHERS
There are a number of causes of feather loss. In very young chicks, the cause is usually *French molt*, which is described elsewhere in the book. *Feather lice* could be the

culprits, with the bird pecking out its feathers because of the intense irritation. Yet another cause could be one of the *skin diseases* caused by molds, such as *ringworm*, described under disease. Should any of these lesions be present, treatment with an antifungal cream should be continued until all signs have disappeared. Except in the case of French molt, if a bird begins to lose feathers or develop bald patches, it should be examined carefully for any skin trouble. If none is apparent, then lice should be suspected and the recommended treatment carried out.

LUTINOS

A lutino is a bird of the green series with the addition of an ino gene. This masks the underlying color, leaving a bird of an allover vivid yellow color. The object of all lutino breeders, having achieved a high standard of show-style budgerigars, is to improve the color until it reaches an almost orangy shade known as "hot yellow." The lutino is one of the sex-linked variety of birds. It has red eyes with white iris rings and the legs and feet are a fleshy pink.

M

MARKINGS

In some varieties certain markings must be present to comply with the standard for the variety; in other varieties, certain of the markings must be absent or almost invisible. To become a successful exhibitor of a variety, it is important that the breeder learns about those markings which apply to that variety. To become a judge, all the stipulations for color and markings must be assimilated. All the standards are given in the Standard of Perfection book of the American Budgerigar Society in the US, or in the publications of the relevant ruling bodies in other countries.

MASK

Ideally, the face of a show budgerigar should be the size of a circle 2.5 cm (1 in) in diameter. The lower part of the face, below the beak, is known as the mask. In the green series birds it is yellow, and in the blue series (except the yellow face blues) it is white.

The depth of color undoubtedly enhances the mask, which can, on occasions, be too pale. It should be

A multi-spotted opaline budgerigar with an untrimmed mask.

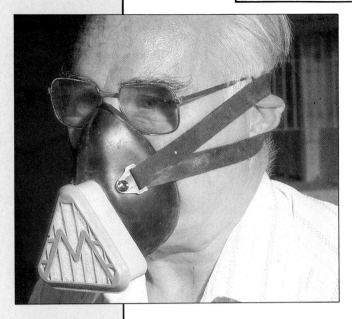

A protective mask is recommended to anyone with asthma or other breathing or chest ailments.

A budgerigar cock which has had its mask trimmed ready for a show. This task should be done a few days before exhibiting the birds to allow the feathers to settle.

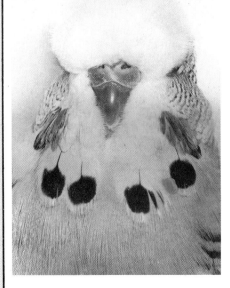

wide and deep, with six evenly spaced round spots at the lower edge.

MASKS, PROTECTIVE

Dust from budgerigars kept in large numbers can be irritating to some breeders' lungs. Dust particles of a reasonable size are usually trapped by the cilia in the nose or upper respiratory tract and are coughed or blown away, but small particles can be inhaled and the tiniest particles can reach the alveoli of the lungs where they can cause trouble. Anyone who suffers from asthma or other breathing problems or chest diseases is advised to wear a mask when

cleaning out cages and flights where a lot of dust is created. The mask covers the nose and mouth, but allows easy breathing. Spraying the floors of flights, nest boxes or other areas with water before cleaning, helps to combat the dust problem.

MATING

Sometimes mating can be observed in the nursery flight when the youngsters are only ten weeks old, whereas when breeding-fit birds are first put into the breeding cages, it is not uncommon for a pair to mate within minutes. Conversely, some pairs, while successful in breeding, are never seen to mate.

Mating normally takes place on the perch. The hen lies across the perch, making her back concave and lifting her tail so that the feathering around the vent is opened, avoiding any obstruction. The cock mounts onto the back of the hen, arching his back and positioning his tail below hers. After a successful act of copulation, the cock returns to his perch, while the hen remains motionless for a few seconds. Mating usually takes place in the early morning, as soon as the lights are turned on, and it is not uncommon for a pair to mate several times.

MEDICINES

There are many simple types of medicines which can be given to cage birds for a number of complaints, but the inexperienced should never "try" *antibiotics* for which they know neither the dosage nor the specific use. If warmth and simple medicines do not effect a speedy improvement in a sick bird, the professional advice of an avian veterinarian should be sought.

If a bird cuts itself on a sharp piece of metal or wire, the small wound can become infected and an abscess will result. *Tincture of iodine* painted on twice a day, will often cause these little abscesses to disappear. Should they remain, bathing the affected part for five or ten minutes with fairly hot water to which has been added a little iodine may cause the abscess to burst. If this doesn't happen and the swelling has come to a head, it should be pricked with a sterile needle and carefully washed with salt and warm water until it is clean. A little *penicillin ointment*, applied twice daily, will ensure clean healing.

A bird with a *cold* or *cough* shows similar symptoms to a human. The nostrils exude mucous, the eyes sometimes water, the breathing is wheezy and the bird looks fluffed up and generally sorry for itself. It should be kept isolated in a warm place and seven or eight drops of a pleasant-tasting cough medicine, such as that sold for human babies, can be added to its drinking water.

A useful medicine to keep in the aviary medicine chest is *cold*, *black*, *unsugared tea* for simple *diarrhea*. Alf Ormerod, one of the world's most experienced breeders, states that it should be made by first using a tea bag in the normal way – and then drinking the tea yourself. Then use the tea bag for the second time, to make a strong infusion to be used in place of water for the sick bird. Unless this is kept in a refrigerator, the mixture should be thrown away and a new supply made quite frequently.

Other medicines which should be kept in the birds' medicine box are sulphur ointment for the treatment of *scaly face* or *scaly leg*. Ordinary eye lotion or tablets, as sold for humans, can be kept for use as eye drops for eyes which are red and which are obviously causing the bird discomfort. The cause of this is often a tiny piece of seed husk or sand which has slipped under the lid, or else the bird may have been in a draft. A miniature bottle of brandy is useful for birds which have a chill or have been badly frightened. Six drops are added to three tablespoons of water and used in the drinker.

Two antibiotic creams which are very useful, but have to be obtained under prescription from a doctor or vet, are Terramycin Ophthalmic, which is very effective against any *pus-forming organisms* and useful for *sinusitis*, and penicillin ointment for use on any *infected wounds*.

Budgerigars often suffer from *iodine deficiency* and a course of extra iodine is useful. Care must be taken not to overdose; two drops in 0.5 liter (1 pt) of water is all that is needed. The treatment should be continued for three weeks for maximum benefit.

A small bottle of a multivitamin perparation is useful as a tonic and is valuable for use after a bird has been treated with an antibiotic.

Liquid paraffin, for use if *egg-binding* occurs or as a mild laxative, is useful.

Sucrose added to the water also acts as a mild purgative if a bird is *constipated*.

MENDELIAN THEORY
Around 1860, long before genes had been discovered, Gregor Mendel, an Austrian monk, conducted a series of tests using garden peas. He crossed dwarf peas with tall peas and produced all tall peas; he self-pollinated these and produced 75 percent tall and 25 percent dwarf. Self-pollinating again, he found all the dwarf variety bred true: 30 percent of the tall variety bred true and the remainder of the tall variety gave 75 percent tall and 25 percent dwarf again. He continued with these experiments and added further complications. He saw that some of the plants had green seed, while others had wrinkled and yellow seeds. He produced tables showing that some varieties were dominant and others recessive. He proved that although two varieties could be of the visual dominant variety, if they were both carrying the recessive feature in a hidden or split form, the two recessives could join together and produce a plant or a seed of the recessive variety. In all, Mendel studied seven pairs of characters in peas, all of which proved that his original theories were correct. Sixty-five years later, two scientists who were also greatly interested in budgerigars, Dr. H. Duncker and Consul General Cremer of Germany, applied

A humane mouse-catching device. Once the mice have entered, they cannot escape and can later be released, unharmed, into the countryside or park.

magnesium, phosphorus, sulphur and potassium are all found in budgerigar seeds; iron is found in greens, in wholegrain bread, oats and eggs; sodium and chloride are obtainable from oats, bread and cuttlefish. The only mineral necessary for health, which does not occur naturally in the budgerigar's diet, appears to be iodine and that can be supplied by iodine pellets or through seed soaked in a very mild solution of iodine.

MIRRORS

If, for any reason, a pet bird has to be left in a cage without company for any length of time, there is no doubt that it becomes lonely, and the best substitute for its owner/companion is a mirror. It will talk to its mirror, play with its mirror and feed its mirror (for this reason the mirror must be frequently washed). Mirrors of all sizes, with bells or other toys attached, can be bought from pet shops. The wisest choice is a mirror made from polished steel, because if this is pulled out and dropped in play, it will not break leaving minute slivers of glass lying on the floor.

Mendel's theories to color in budgerigars and produced tables giving the expectations from every possible mating of budgerigars known at that time. These tables are still in use today, listed in the Budgerigar Society book *Budgerigar Matings and Colour Expectations* which is available from the American Budgerigar Society.

MICE

Mice and budgerigars do not coexist in harmony. The droppings and urine of the rodents are poisonous to the birds, and mice have even been known to nibble off the feet of tiny babies. Every sensible precaution should be taken to ensure that mice never get into a birdroom or flight and that no seed or foodstuff is contaminated by their excreta. If any sign of mice is found, their source of ingress should be discovered and blocked as quickly as possible and every mouse inside the birdhouse caught and destroyed. Traps for this purpose are widely advertised in the birdworld press.

MINERALS

Most of the mineral requirements of a budgerigar are contained in its normal diet. Manganese,

MITE

The most common variety of mite which can infest breeding establishments is the *red mite* or *roost mite*. During the day it is grey in color and hides in cracks and crevices or under nest-box blocks. At night, the bloodsucking creatures emerge to gorge on the blood of the birds. The poor hen sitting in the nest box and the young chicks are favorite targets. These bloodsucking forays of the agile mite can cause serious *anemia* and loss of weight. When there is bad infestation, an early morning visit, when lights first go on, may show patches of blood-filled bright red mites which have not had time to scuttle away to their daytime hideaways. The mite can be brought into the aviary by new stock, or can come from wild birds perching on the wires and shedding a few of their mites, which very quickly multiply.

No pet owners or budgerigar

White blue cock.

A Capern's card
showing a dark green
budgerigar.

Light green
dominant pied cock
showing a clear
yellow band just
above the thighs.

Opaline light green
dominant pied cock
with an exceptionally
high frontal rise.

Eye-catching varieties

Dark green
dominant pied cock

breeders will want their birds to become infested with these bloodsucking parasites, and prevention is better than cure. The mites will not live long if all the breeding cages have been thoroughly sprayed with an *acaricide*, or a preparation containing hexachloride, malathion, pyrethrum or derris root, or a combination of these, and then coated with paint impregnated with the same.

If red mites are found, the birds should be caught up, very quickly sprayed with one of the proprietary mite-killing sprays which are harmless to birds or chicks (pyrethrum-based sprays are the safest kind), and transferred to a clean cage which has first been sprayed with an anti-mite preparation and given a new nest

box. The old nest box should be emptied and the sawdust or other litter burned. The nest box can then be thoroughly soaked, disinfected and treated with an anti-mite preparation before reuse. The husks and litter from the breeding cage should also be burned and the perches and inside of the cage scrubbed with a strong solution of disinfectant and then treated with a spray containing an anti-mite preparation. Careful watch must be kept on all adjacent cages, because red mites are agile, long-legged creatures which very quickly migrate to pastures new. They can live for a long time – a matter of months – away from their unwitting hosts and without a feed of blood. Constant watchfulness is necessary until the end of the breeding season, when the breeding room can be emptied and thoroughly mite-proofed

MOLTING

A soft molt can occur at any time of the year. It can be brought on by a change in the weather; it can occur when the birds are first put back into the flights after the breeding season; it can happen immediately after a show, when the birds have been taken to a hall where the temperature is totally different from that of their normal environment. In a soft molt, the bird loses a number of feathers, but very seldom the main flights or tail feathers.

At about four months of age, a baby budgerigar goes through its first molt. In the normal varieties, it loses all the "baby" feathers from above the beak to the top of its head. The new feathers which grow are of a clear color with none of the baby *striations* or bars, and at the same time the white iris rings appear around the pupils of its eyes. When the new feathers regrow, they are usually a deeper color than the nest feathers.

In a pet bird, where the temperature of its environment is kept almost even throughout the year, the molt can occur at any time, but often takes place in late spring or early summer when central heating is first turned off, creating a different, sometimes cooler, temperature for a while.

The main, or annual, molt usually takes place in the autumn. The commencement can differ by as much as six weeks from the north of the country to the south, but as soon as the temperatures begin to drop the birds begin to lose feathers. They take between six and eight weeks to complete this molt. The first sign of the molt is that the birds lose body weight, then feathers, and at this time they are more susceptible to catching colds and chills. At the very first sign of the beginning of the annual molt, the birds should be fed with seed which has been treated with cod liver oil emulsion (see *FEEDING*). During this stage, the birds need good wholesome seed, some millet sprays as a tidbit, and plenty of rest and quiet. *Calcium* should always be available in the form of cuttlefish and grit.

Additional hours of artificial light seem to hasten the process of the molt, but it is not advised because then it seems not to be quite complete. If the birds are "forced" through the molt, their bodies seem not to be fully and naturally prepared for the rigors of early breeding, whereas if they are allowed only natural daylight during September and October, they seem to lose more feathers and then come through into tiptop breeding condition. As they begin to grow new feathers, their activity increases. Although they are not fully feather-fit for showing, their extra activity shows that the molt is almost over and they are beginning to come into breeding condition.

Sometimes a bird will molt very severely and lose a number of flight feathers at the same time, causing it to experience difficulty in flying. Any birds in this condition should be caught and caged in stock cages.

If it is desired to delay the molt of show birds in very good condition, they should be regularly sprayed with tepid water. This is, however, a temporary measure.

MUTATIONS

Although it seems incredible when one attends a bird show and sees the miscellany of colors and varieties of budgerigars on display, all of them are descended from the original wild green Australian birds which were first introduced into the UK in the early 1840s. Some of the mutations occurred in the wild, but many of them have occurred in private birdrooms and aviaries.

Surprisingly, when these new mutations appear in one stud, they often happen simultaneously in another, sometimes in a different country. When a new mutation first appears, the birds are zealously sought after and the prices charged can be phenomenal. Skyblues, greywings, clearwings, lutinos and pieds all commanded high prices when they first appeared. The newest mutation to become popular is the spangle, but news is being received from Australia of brownwings and other new varieties. Two mutations which have not appeared naturally, but which many breeders have attempted to produce, are an all-black or black-winged bird, and the red budgerigar.

N

NEST BOXES

For many years after budgerigars were introduced into the UK, nest boxes were made from empty coconut shells with a hole cut for the birds to go in and out. While the birds obviously found these satisfactory, the same could hardly be said for the breeder, who had no idea of how many eggs were laid or whether they were fertile, until he or she saw the youngsters leave the nest.

Nest boxes now can be found in a variety of shapes and sizes and are normally made of plywood or softwood. The latter is recommended, particularly that used for floorboards: it helps to absorb moisture when the chicks are growing and it has good insulating properties which helps to keep the nest box warm. The hen can chew at the box with no fear that she might eat glue which can happen when plywood is used. An ideal size is 30 × 21.5 × 16.5 cm (12 × 8½ × 7¼ in) externally.

Carpentry skills do not need to be of a high standard to construct these nest boxes. It is, in effect, a room for the hen, a room in which she must feel secure, for she will spend many hours at a stretch sitting or sleeping in the nest box. To make a simple box with a let-down front, cut two pieces of lumber, 30 × 21.5 cm (12 × 8½ in) for the back and front, two pieces 30 × 14.5 cm (12 × 5⅝ in) for the top and bottom, and two side pieces of 17 × 14.5 cm (6⅞ × 5⅝ in). If the box is to be hung onto the front of the cage, an entrance hole, on a level with the space cut from the wire front, should be cut in the back panel. The hole should not be so large as to make the hen feel insecure, nor so small that she might damage herself while going in and out of the box. About 4 cm (1¾ in) is the right size for the normal show bird.

The cinnamon factor

Opaline cinnamon grey cock.

box can give the same thrill as a budgie greeting you with a happy tune when you return to your home, and it will be a source of constant amusement to callers.

TAMING

Confidence is the secret of taming a budgerigar. The finest form of training is done as soon as the baby leaves the nest box, and pet breeders can almost ensure being able to sell their youngsters if they, or one of their family, is prepared to spend the time and take the trouble to play with the baby budgerigars and hand feed them until they have no fear whatsoever of people and hands. Just as the chicks once scrambled back into the nest box, so they will scramble through a hole made with finger and thumb, and if they are used to sitting on a hand and eating seed or millet spray from it, they will have no fear when a hand is put into their new pet cage.

Because a pet cage is very different from the stock cage from which most budgies are taken, they should be left alone for a few hours to acclimatize themselves with their new surroundings. It is best not to have a swing in the cage for the first day or two, so that they can learn to fly confidently to a perch, knowing that they can land on it safely. The swing, if there is one, can be introduced once the bird feels quite safe in the cage. Open dishes on the bottom of the cage for seed, or even seed sprinkled over the bottom of the cage is advisable for the first two or three days, until the baby bird is used to eating out of the new seed containers. If the new owner has the patience to sit with his or her hand inside the cage, holding a millet spray, the bird, even if it has not been reared as a pet, will begin to eat the seeds from it after a while and the more this is done, the sooner the bird becomes used to, and eventually starts to sit on, the hand. A budgerigar cannot be said to be tame until it will hop onto the owner's hand with the same alacrity as it will hop onto a perch. Once it has lost its initial fear of a hand being put into the

cage, it can be coaxed onto the hand by putting the finger just underneath its chest, in front of its legs and slowly pressing the finger backwards. As it must perch, and it can no longer hold on to the real perch, it automatically moves onto the finger, hardly realizing that its perch has changed.

Some birds are far more nervous than others and will fly wildly if someone approaches their cage at the beginning. All movements should be slow and unhurried, and the owner should talk to the bird as he or she approaches the cage. A little patience at this stage will be well rewarded later on. Once the budgerigar is hand tame, and will hop onto a finger automatically when it is put inside the cage, the bird can be allowed out into the room – after any open or electric fire has been covered and the drapes have been closed to prevent it from flying into the unfamiliar glass pane. Slowly it can be taught to perch on a shoulder, by being transferred from finger to shoulder or to another person's shoulder. Soon, it will accept a shoulder as another of its perches and it will fly from cage to shoulder as soon as it is allowed out. The tamer a budgie becomes, the more responsibility the owner has to ensure that he or she *never* leaves the house with the bird still on a shoulder, and *never* opens the cage before first checking that all doors and windows are closed. So much heartbreak has been caused by a bird being taken outdoors, or getting out, and then being startled and flying off wildly. Once out into the outside world it is lost, frightened and often flies a long distance before alighting, by which time it is far away from home.

Unless a hawk or other hunting bird is in the vicinity, the ordinary garden birds do not attack the lone budgerigar, but it has no knowledge of cats and often falls victim to them, and in any case it has been used to eating only seed and there is very little seed in the wild except seeding grasses which are only available at certain times of the year and, unfortunately, have often been treated with sprays which could be lethal. The escaped bird is unlikely to survive for long.

TICKING

Ticking, frosting and flecking are all words used to describe excess *melanin* which causes marks on top of the head of budgerigars. It is a fault in show birds and is penalized by the judges. An illustration of this will be found under the heading *FLECKING*.

This fault is a problem because it is hereditary, and it is therefore wiser not to breed with birds which are flecked. Although by judicious breeding the fault can apparently be made to disappear, it can, and often is, carried by the offspring in a recessive and hidden form and will reappear in future generations. Unless the birds are of otherwise superb quality, it is better not to use flecked birds in the breeding team, and no one but the really experienced breeder should use them under any circumstances.

TOENAILS

When in the nest box, the toes of baby budgerigars may become fouled by excreta and often, by the time the nest box is examined, this has become quite hard. It should not be picked off while hard, as it is very easy to pull off a toenail. As well as causing the bird some pain and disfiguration, the bird will thus be spoiled for showing. The foot should be soaked in warm water for a few seconds to soften the excreta which can then be removed with a soft cloth.

Like human nails, the bird's toenails grow. Provided it has access to some sort of rough surface and has something other than round doweling for perches, normal moving around will wear away the small amount of growth, but sometimes a hen, sitting for a long time in a nest box, will grow excessively long toenails. These are a nuisance for the bird and can also accidentally pierce an egg, causing the chick inside to die before it is born. Pets are prone to overgrown toenails, partly because they usually live to a ripe old age and partly because they lead a less active life than a bird in an aviary. One thing which will help to prevent this is a piece of old brick left in the corner of the cage. They use this as a form of grit and for entertainment in scraping it away to nothing, and as they hold it in one foot, or press a foot against it to be able to pull it apart more successfully, it keeps their nails trimmed.

If toenails do become too long, they have to be cut. This causes no more pain to the budgie than it does to the human. The foot should be held up to the light where it will be seen that blood vessels grow part of the way down the toe and then there is a part which is purely nail and is devoid of any blood vessels. Cut a little at a time with sharp nail clippers, holding the toe up to the light each time to make sure you will not cut the living part. Continue with each of the toes in turn. Once cutting

A rotating swing is a favorite of budgerigars. This example is sold commercially, but it is also easy to make for oneself.

has been commenced, the nails will grow quicker than they did before, and so will need to be cut on a regular basis for the rest of the bird's life.

If, by some unfortunate chance, the nail is cut too deep and bleeding occurs, a little styptic pencil will often stop the bleeding. This should be followed by a drop of salt water to remove the silver nitrate from the pencil. The bird should then be kept quiet in its cage for a while to prevent the bleeding starting again or, if it has not been stopped, to give the blood time to clot and stop of its own accord.

A budgerigar with bell and mirror.

TOYS
Budgies are naturally playful and, even in flights with many others, they love to swing on homemade swings (see *EQUIPMENT*). They also make their own playthings from feathers which have molted, millet spray stalks and greens which have been eaten down to the stalks.

Pets have no other birds with which to play and appreciate toys with which to amuse themselves. Owners should check these toys just as carefully as they check those for children's use, because the clanger from a bell which is loose can be swallowed by the budgie just as easily as a child will swallow a loose bead, while a piece of wire sticking out can cause the same damage to either. Mirrors are almost a necessity for a happy budgie and a particular favorite is a mirror at the bottom of a shallow dish filled with water. The budgie will splash around happily in this – but splash is the operative word! The dish should be placed on newspaper or an old cloth; otherwise most of the water will land on the carpet.

Kelly dolls are another favorite, and provided the owner has the patience to pick them up from the floor a hundred times a day, the budgie will cheerfully continue to throw them over. Care must be taken that the rungs of ladders are not so far apart that the budgie can get stuck between them.

If storebought toys are not available, several empty spools strung tightly on a string are well received, although it is often necessary to renew the string, which will be chewed through. Another item enjoyed by most budgies is a shallow tray on which have been placed a few glass marbles. The bird will spend hours on end throwing these out onto the floor.

TRACE MINERALS
In addition to the proteins, carbohydrates and fats which the birds obtain from seed and the various additives which are given to them, they also require a small quantity of certain trace minerals for their health and well-being. Most of these are contained in canary and millet seed, but there is often insufficient calcium and iodine in the normal diet.

Iodine can be given in the form of iodine pellets, but because of the budgerigar's habit of tearing at any object which is easily crumbled, many of these are wasted. Pet stores stock a harder, larger block containing iodine which, although marketed for pigeons, is ideal for budgerigar breeding cages or flights, though

Budgerigars like to climb ladders but make certain that the bird cannot become stuck between the rungs.

love to have branches of trees to play in and with and to eat the leaves, bark and, if soft enough, the wood itself. Most trees are suitable, but yew, laburnum and other poisonous species must be avoided at all costs. The favorites are the fruit trees, unless one is lucky enough to be able to grow a eucalyptus tree. In Australia, where the eucalyptus trees grow wild, budgies descend upon them like locusts, eating leaves, bark and wood and often nesting in the trunks of dead trees. The fanciers who have succeeded in growing eucalyptus elsewhere find the birds attack any newly picked branches with great enthusiasm.

TYPE
The term type embodies the whole image of the bird. The bird should be standing on the perch with a backline of 30 degrees from the vertical. The head must be held in a bold, confident manner. The wings must be held tightly to the body with the tips of the wings just cushioning the tail. If the bird has a very slight, very gentle dip in the back line, it does seem to give it a more desirable stance and to make it look more alert, but, when viewed from either side, the line must be clean and sweeping from head to tail with the maximum width around the breast and shoulder area. Even if the bird has long feathering, it should be tight and in place. Coarse-feathered birds are often criticized for lack of type because the feathers, being long, tend to be loose.

Balance is an integral part of type. Everything must be in proportion. The body must be in proportion to the head, the mask in proportion to the head, the spots in proportion to the mask and the beak in proportion to the face. A budgerigar with a small body and big head can look like a hanging parrot; with a big body and small head, it resembles a pigeon slumped across the perch. A really well-balanced budgerigar is a thing of beauty – it is a bird with type!

too large for the pet cage. Iodine can also be given in the water, but in quite minute quantities, or a few drops of a well-known iodine-based disinfectant can be added to the water. Alternatively, millet sprays can be soaked in a weak solution of iodine-treated water before being fed to the birds.

Oystershell and limestone grit are the most readily available forms of calcium, but vitamin D is also necessary for the absorption of calcium by the body. Vitamin D is manufactured by the body when it is exposed to sunlight, but as few breeding cages obtain any direct sunlight, it is vital, particularly at the time when calcium is needed by the hen for making eggshell, and by the chicks to make strong bones, to give extra vitamin D. This is available in cod liver oil which can be mixed with the seed given.

TREES
A tree-planted aviary is not suitable for budgerigars, or to be more accurate, budgerigars are not suitable for a tree-planted aviary. Their habit of tearing to shreds anything which can be torn is hardly conducive to the survival of trees and plants. However, they

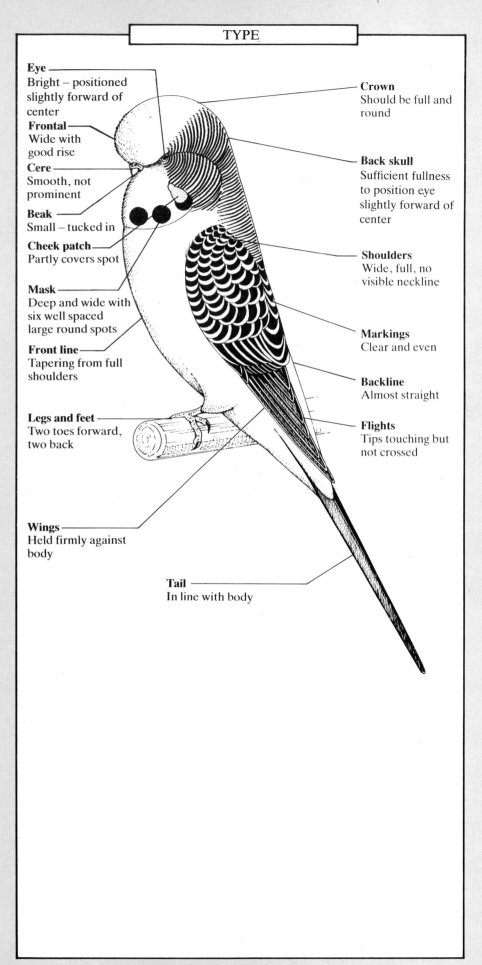

Eye
Bright – positioned slightly forward of center

Frontal
Wide with good rise

Cere
Smooth, not prominent

Beak
Small – tucked in

Cheek patch
Partly covers spot

Mask
Deep and wide with six well spaced large round spots

Front line
Tapering from full shoulders

Legs and feet
Two toes forward, two back

Wings
Held firmly against body

Tail
In line with body

Crown
Should be full and round

Back skull
Sufficient fullness to position eye slightly forward of center

Shoulders
Wide, full, no visible neckline

Markings
Clear and even

Backline
Almost straight

Flights
Tips touching but not crossed

U

UNDERSHOT BEAK

This is a deformity of the beak caused by food being caught under the upper hook of the mandible of chicks in the nest box. As this hardens, the lower mandible is unable to fit underneath. Unless the top beak is cleaned regularly, the soft food sets like concrete and eventually the lower mandible passes over instead of under the

A case of an undershot beak.

top hook. Not only does this disfigure the bird, but it also causes difficulty in cracking seed. To assist the bird in eating properly, the lower mandible needs to be trimmed. This is best carried out with strong, sharp nail clippers and care must be taken not to cut into the blood supply. If the bird is held up to the light, the end of the blood vessel region can be seen quite clearly and any cutting must not go into or beyond this area. It is best to take off the excess a little at a time, checking regularly to ensure that the bloodline has not been reached. Beginners are recommended to ask the help of an experienced fancier the first time this operation is necessary, as it is easier to learn by watching it being done.

USEFUL ADDRESSES

The newcomer to budgerigars is often at a loss where to look for help, where to find the address of his local club or of other fanciers in his area. The American Budgerigar Society, the Budgerigar Society or area societies in Britain, and the ruling bodies in other countries can supply these details. The addresses of these bodies follow:

AUSTRALIA – Budgerigar Society of South Australia. Mr. R. Deslandes, No. 7 West Street, Ascot Park, South Australia, 5043.

BELGIUM – Ornitho Club Seraing, 2 Rue des Steches, 4230 Horion Hosemont, Belgium.

CANADA – The Budgerigar and Foreign Bird Society of Canada Inc., c/o Mr. L. Lavalette, 126 Greyabbey Trail, West Hill, Ontario, Canada MIE 1Vg. Southern Alberta Budgerigar and Cage Bird Society, c/o Mr. V. Bugala, 239–20th Ave., N.W., Calgary, Alberta, Canada. T2M 1C3.

EIRE – Eire Budgerigar Society, Hon. Sec. Mr. H. Harrison, Rocky Valley Lodge, Kilmacanugue, Co. Wicklow, Eire.

FRANCE – Club Nationale Des Oiseaux Exotiques. Mr. J. Barre, Lot. No. 17, Champ de Rochefort, 16400 Puymoyen, France.

GERMANY – Austauschzentrale der Vogel-liebhaber und -züchter Deutschlands E.V., General Sekretar: G. Wittenbrock, 286 Osterholz-Scharmbeck, vor Der Elm 1, Munchen 246 74 807, Germany.
Redaktion D.S.V. Nachrichten, Schildsheider Str., 4006 Erkrath 2, Germany.

JAPAN – The Japan International Budgerigar Association, Secretary Mr. M. Takezawa, 16-24-2 Chome, Nozato, Nishiyodogawa, Osaka 555, Japan.
The Japan Budgerigar Club, Mr. H. Nakayama, 3-6 Nishiyama 1 Chome, Kashlwa Si, Chiba Ken, 277 Japan.

THE NETHERLANDS (HOLLAND) – For full information regarding the various societies, contact "Onze Vogels" P.O. Box 74, Bergen op Zoom, The Netherlands.

NEW ZEALAND – The Budgerigar Society of New Zealand, Secretary: Mrs. C. R. Carlyon, P. O. Box 54-077, Plimmerton, Wellington, New Zealand.

SWEDEN – The Swedish Budgerigar Society, Secretary Mr. U. Thorn, Bjornidegrand 11, S 162 46 Vallingby, Sweden.

UNITED KINGDOM – The Budgerigar Society, 49/53 Hazelwood Road, Northampton NN1 1LG, England.

Clearwing Budgerigar Breeders' Association, c/o M. Freemantle, 15 Northcourt Avenue, Reading, England.

Crested Budgerigar Club, c/o Mr. and Mrs. Risebrow, 59 Glencoe Rd., Ipswich, Suffolk, England.

Lutino and Albino Breeders' Society, c/o J. Bancroft, 14 Whitehouse Drive, Long Stratton, Norfolk, England.

Rare Variety and Colour Budgerigar Society, c/o C. Putt, 124 Stonewall Crescent, Whitestone, Nuneaton, Warwicks, England.

Spangled Budgerigar Breeders' Association c/o J. Canham, 30 New Road, Mepal, Nr. Ely, Cambridgeshire, England.

Variegated Budgerigar Club, c/o Mr. & Mrs. J. Suddell, "Southdene" 218 Noak Hill Road, Billericay, Essex, England.

UNITED STATES – The American Budgerigar Society, Secretary, Mrs. Natalie Pittman, 1704 Kangaroo, Kileen, Texas 76543, or Chairman, Ms. Ermafern Collins, 304 Kellogg, Dallas Center, Idaho 50063.

District 1 – John Palumbo, 169 Hooker Road, Bridgeport, Connecticut 06610.

District 2 – Catherine Stec, 3862 Franklin Park Drive, Stirling Heights, Michigan 48078.

District 3 – Toni Mancini, 29 Summershade Circle, Piscataway, New Jersey 08854.

District 4 – Allan J. Jakubowski, 5356 North 25th Street, Glendale, Wisconsin 53209.

District 5 – Sherrill Capi, 3300 North East 56th Court, Fort Lauderdale, Florida 33308.

District 6 – Robert L. Howard Jr., RT2 Box 34H, Franklington, Louisiana 70438.

District 7 – Rod Hatcher, 610 Quebec Street, New Virginia, Iowa 50210.

District 8 – Dr. Mitch Funderburk, 16914 High Noon Road, Del Valle, Texas 78617.

District 9 – Tom Lams, 4348 La Cosa Avenue, Fremont, California 94536.

District 10 – Charles "Jack" Chapman, 373 Corto Street, Ojai, California 93023.

District 11 – Patricia Gibson, 10537 Steel Trace Court, Charlotte, North Carolina 28210.

(For details of states covered by the various districts, see **FANCY**.)

VARIEGATED
This term is used to describe the irregular patches of color on the body and wings and the lack of color in the flight feathers of the pied variety of budgerigars.

VARIETIES
There are now a large variety of budgerigars obtainable. The *normal* varieties include light, dark and olive green, grey green, light, dark and olive yellow, grey yellow, yellow suffused, skyblue, cobalt, mauve, violet, grey, and white suffused. The same list of colors is available in the *opaline, cinnamon* and the *opaline cinnamon* varieties. The next series are the *greywings*, which come in all the basic colors followed by *opaline greywings*. In the *clearwing* variety there are yellow-wing light, dark and olive greens, yellow-wing grey greens, whitewing skyblues, whitewing cobalts, whitewing mauves, whitewing violets and whitewing greys. The whole series of colors is repeated in the *fallow* variety, the *dominant* and *recessive pieds*, the *clearflights*, *crests* and the new *spangles*. In addition to these there are *albinos, lutinos, lacewings yellows* and *whites*, and *dark-eyed yellows and whites* There are well over 100 different varieties from which to choose, whereas at the beginning of the century the choice was light green or yellow.

VENTILATION
Adequate ventilation is an absolute essential in the birdroom for the well-being of your stock, while drafts must be avoided at all costs. The recommended form of ventilation is a series of mouseproof air vents fitted into the walls low down, preferably beneath the bottom layer of breeding cages, combined with louvers or an exhaust fan fitted as high in the birdroom as possible. Whichever is

used must be fitted with a birdproof screen across the opening just in case any of the birds escape from the cages into the main room. This ensures a constant flow of fresh air which also helps to carry out some of the dust.

VERMIN
The urine and droppings of rats and mice are poisonous to the birds. If vermin are present in an aviary, seed, sawdust, shavings, cuttlefish, anything with which the birds will come in contact, can be fouled by their urine without the breeder being able to see any trace. If any of these items are fed to the budgerigars, or used anywhere where the birds can chew or nibble at them, the results could be disastrous. Prevention, in this case, is far better than cure. When the birdhouse is being built, every precaution should be taken to make the building mouseproof (if it is mouseproof it will certainly be ratproof). Small-mesh wire should be fitted over every means of entrance. Seed should never be left around in half-opened sacks, but stored in plastic dustbins or similar containers. No foodstuffs should be stored in dark, fairly inaccessible cupboards at floor level, but kept on shelves, in sight. Feeding trays are best mounted on plastic or smooth-sided material so that mice cannot crawl up. Seed should never be purchased from a shop where open sacks are left around; it is far better to buy a complete sack and store it until it is needed. If, despite every precaution, traces of vermin are found in the birdroom, they must be eradicated as quickly as possible. There are a number of patent traps for this purpose, which are safe for birds, advertised in the fancy press. Poison bait is *not* a good idea.

VITAMINS
Budgerigars need vitamins, as does any other form of living creatures, but they need them in minute quantities. Unfortunately, some breeders, in their desire to ensure that their birds have every additive which can be given, overdose their

birds with vitamins, sometimes with unhappy results. An excess of vitamin A has been blamed for some forms of "*going light.*" Vitamin D, in excess, can cause enlarged joints and constipation, among other things. If the diet consists of good wholesome seed, which has been treated with cod liver oil emulsion during the molt and breeding season, an adequate supply of greens and mixed grits, which contain oystershell and limestone, this should take care of the birds' vitamin requirements. Where greens are not available, or not supplied for some reason, a few drops of a multivitamin product for birds can be added to the water, but this should be added at only about five drops to 0.5 liter (1 pt).

Budgerigars obtain vitamin B12 by eating their own dried droppings, but after any illness which has caused diarrhea, these are not available, nor is vitamin B12 present in the droppings if antibiotics have been administered for a period. This shortage can be made up by adding something like Avitron to the water at the rate of one teaspoon per 0.5 liter (1 pt). The other vitamin lacking in most natural foods is vitamin E, which is very beneficial during the breeding season. A small quantity of bee pollen added to the softfood fills this need.

WASHING

In country areas, or places where the air is clean and clear, there is seldom any need to wash budgerigars for showing, but in cities or highly polluted atmospheres, spraying is not really sufficient to clean the feathers, and the birds, particularly the lighter varieties, such as lutinos, albinos, clearwings and lacewings, do need to be washed. This should always be carried out in the morning, to allow the birds all day to dry naturally. Most breeders choose a weekend for this rather lengthy task. The birds are washed about a month before the show and then put into clean stock cages to dry. As they are then kept indoors in the stock cages, light spraying will keep their feathers in a clean condition, ready for the show.

To wash a bird, or birds, three bowls are required. The first contains warm water and baby shampoo, the second plain warm water, and the third warm water with the addition of a few drops of plume conditioner (this is optional). The bird is held so that its eyes are protected and the

The correct way to hold a budgerigar when bathing it.

141

washing carried out with an old soft shaving brush, always brushing in the direction in which the feathers grow. Should there be any staining around the beak, or dried blood spots on top of the head, an old soft toothbrush can be used to remove them. Once the head and body have been washed, each wing should be spread out gently and washed on both sides. The bird is then dipped into the second bowl. The water must not be allowed to cover the head, but only very gently dripped over the head and beak areas. Finally, the bird is dipped into the third basin of water in the same way. Excess water can be blotted off with an old towel before the bird is released into the clean stock cage.

WATER

Although budgies do not drink a great deal, a supply of *fresh* water must always be available. With an automatic system, it is assured that the water is just as fresh as the water drunk by humans, because it comes straight from the tap. If this is not available, then the water should be changed every day. In cages, the most convenient form of water container is the fountain drinker, which consists of a clear plastic tube with an open end. When the tube is filled, a cap with a drinking spout is fitted and the fountain turned upside down. The force of gravity fills the drinking spout, allowing the birds to drink at will. Care must be taken not to fit the cap with the cutout piece meeting the cutout on the tube, otherwise the water would run out when it was fitted to the cage, leaving the bird with only the few drops remaining in the spout. If the spout becomes contaminated with droppings or seeds, the water quickly becomes foul and should be changed immediately.

For flights or garden aviaries, open dishes are the usual vessels used. The water should be no more than 4 cm (1½ in) deep because the birds use the water dishes as baths and if one became too wet and unable to fly, it could get into difficulties, or even drown. Birds will bathe in any temperature; it is a form of recreation for them and appears to do them no harm, even in midwinter; in fact, it tends to tone up the feathers.

Thought must be given to the position of water dishes. They should not be placed under perches where they could become fouled by droppings, or where husks from the seed are likely to fly into them. Ideally, they should be placed on a pedestal, higher than the food dishes, in a shaded area which will minimize evaporation from the sun and reduce the growth of algae. Glazed dishes are recommended because they are easy to keep clean. In a garden aviary, they can easily be washed using the garden hose, then replenished.

WEANING

Baby budgerigars are usually self-supporting at the age of six weeks and can then be taken away from their parents. If possible, it is as well to take them away in batches, rather than singly. When half a dozen or more youngsters from different families are ready to be separated from their parents and put in a stock cage together, the more forward babies teach the others how to crack seed with ease. Some breeders like to put an old and reliable cock into the cage with the youngsters as a venerable teacher, but this can have its difficulties if the cock begins to attack one or more of the youngsters. Generally, the chicks manage quite well on their own.

During the first few weeks of their independent life, the babies should be given the same additives that they have been used to in the breeding cage. Soaked oats, soaked mung beans and softfood are always welcomed, as are millet sprays. Chickweed is greeted with delight if it is available, and another very good source of vitamins is spinach.

If, within 24 hours, it is observed that a baby is not feeding and the crop feels empty, it can be put back with its parents or with foster parents, but a close watch must be kept on it for a couple of hours to make certain that the parents do not reject and attack it. If this happens and the parents will not feed it, and the baby is unable to feed itself, the breeder will have to try hand feeding (see *HAND FEEDING*). Fortunately, at this stage of development, hand feeding is seldom necessary for more than a day or two and is well worth a try if it saves the youngster. A bird this old can take food from a spoon quite easily and does not need a brooder. In a show cage with seed on the floor, it will soon learn to crack its own food, especially if another, more forward baby is kept in the same cage.

WINGS
The wings of a show budgerigar should be 9.5 cm (3¾ in) long. They should be carried just above the cushion of the tail and should not be crossed. Wings which cross over each other is one of the commonest faults and one for the beginner to avoid when buying his first stock because it is a fault which is difficult to eradicate. Another fault, which makes the bird look most unattractive, is a habit of dropping the wings, or sometimes just one wing, down at the side of the body, looking as if the bird is too tired to hold them up.

Wings, carried correctly, should be neatly folded and look as if they are part of the body.

WRONG CLASS
All officials at every show try to watch for birds which have been entered in the wrong class, as they are anxious for every bird to be judged fairly. If the show secretary or stewards notice a bird has been wrong-classed, they will re-class it correctly. Even the judge will have a bird re-classed if he or she has not yet judged the class in which it should have been entered. In the rush of setting up the show, however, the officials may miss a wrong-classed bird, and if the judge has already passed the class in which the bird should have been entered, then he or she must disqualify it. It is very easy for a novice, with a few blue birds, to see classes on the catalog for "skyblue, cobalt or mauve." As he

has skyblues and cobalts with yellow faces, he enters them in the blue class. What he has failed to do is to read the rest of the classification which tells him that there is a separate class for yellowface blues, and when he arrives at the show he finds his birds disqualified. Another mistake often made is to enter a number of birds, some old and others bred in the current year, and then stick the cage labels for green young onto the green old birds, and so on. Again, they would be marked W/C. Newcomers need to learn what the more experienced have learned, often the hard way, that the classifications on a catalog must be read very, very carefully and the cage tags checked before they are taken to a show to make certain that the right birds are in the right cages.

It is very easy for a novice to mistake an opaline for a normal, not to notice the cinnamon markings, to mistake a grey green for an olive green, and so on, particularly if the cages are being filled in a fairly dark birdroom. Check and check again is the rule to be followed here. If the new exhibitor is unsure, even after checking, that he or she has labeled all the birds correctly, the steward or secretary checking in the birds at the show will help.

XYZ

X CHROMOSOME

X is the sex chromosome. The cock carries two and the hen one. Several of the varieties of budgerigars are *sex-linked*, which means that their potential can only be carried on the X chromosome. This gives the effect that if a hen is carrying that potential, she displays it visually. If, for example, she is carrying a potential for the lutino variety on her single X chromosome, she will be a lutino. If she is not, she cannot carry the lutino potential in hidden or split form because it cannot be on her other chromosome which is a Y chromosome. As the cock carries two X chromosomes, he can be split for lutino or whichever sex-linked variety he is carrying.

YELLOWFACE

The yellowface variety of budgerigars is unusual in several respects. There are two different types, called *mutant I* and *mutant II*. The mutant I birds are blue birds with yellow faces and masks, and the yellow cuts off immediately beneath the mask. In the mutant II variety, the yellow runs right through the body, changing the blue to turquoise. There is a school of thought which states that these birds are not blue birds at all, but green birds in which the yellow-producing pigment has been partially suppressed. Their mode of inheritance is also unusual, because if two single factor yellowface blues are mated together, they can produce perfectly ordinary-looking whitefaced blues, but 50 percent of these will, theoretically, be double factor yellowface blues and when mated to an ordinary whiteface blue, will produce all yellowface young. This can be absolutely amazing to breeders who have no knowledge of the parentage of their stock of blues.

YELLOWS

Yellows, being the recessive form of green, come in the same range of colors: light, dark, olive and grey yellow. In addition there is a *suffused variety* which also comes in light, dark and olive shades. These birds are suffused with a very dilute shade of the color being masked. Another variety of yellow is the dark-eyed clear yellow which is pure yellow throughout, including clear yellow wings. At a quick glance, the bird could be taken for a pale-colored lutino until the dark eyes are observed.

ZYGOTES

A zygote is the first cell of a chick, which contains the necessary double set of chromosomes.